Arguments

Series editor: John Harrison

'As we plunge deeper into the crisis caused by monetarism and militarism, more and more people will be turning to socialist ideas to find out more about socialism and what socialists are saying.

Arguments for Socialism is developing as an essential reading list for the interested as well as the committed and offers a compact library of essential background information and clear analysis.' *Tony Benn*

First published in 1983 by Pluto Press Limited,
The Works, 105a Torriano Avenue,
London NW5 2RX and Pluto Press Australia Limited, PO Box 199,
Leichhardt, New South Wales 2040, Australia

British Library Cataloguing in Publication Data
Ross, John
Thatcher and friends: the anatomy of the Tory party.
—(Arguments for Socialism)
1. Conservative Party
I. Title   II. Series
324.24104   JN1129C7
ISBN 0-86104-5122

Cover designed by Clive Challis A Gr R
Computerset by Promenade Graphics Limited
Block 23a Lansdown Industrial Estate, Cheltenham GL51 8PL
Printed and bound in Great Britain
by Richard Clay (The Chaucer Press) Limited, Bungay, Suffolk

Thatcher and Friends

The Anatomy of the Tory Party

John Ross

Pluto  Press

Contents

Acknowledgements

First and foremost to John Harrison, without whom the book would not have been written. Second to Richard Kuper, for supervising the various drafts of the manuscript and for much editorial help.

John Walker of the Labour Research Department kindly supplied me with additional material on the finances of the Tory Party. Steve Kennedy gave great help in editing and in many other ways. Andrew Gamble and Alan Freeman kindly read most of the manuscript in various forms. Thanks are also due to John Curtice of Nuffield College, who supplied figures for the regional breakdown of the vote in the 1983 election.

New Left Review allowed me to draw on my research on the British economy under Thatcher which will be published by New Left Books in 1984 as *Profits of Thatcherism*.

The journal *International* and the paper *Socialist Action* let me use much material which had originally appeared in their pages.

Most of all Anna, Katey, and Pat Ross all helped in the production of the book. Anna in particular supplied the title for the last sub-section – which could almost be taken as the theme of the whole book.

It should be stressed that none of the above has any responsibility for errors either of interpretation or fact in what follows.

Introduction: British Politics in the 1980s

The June 1983 General Election was one of the most spectacular in its outcome in British history. The Conservative Party gained a landslide of seats in Parliament, Labour saw its vote fall to the lowest level for 65 years, and the SDP–Liberal Alliance gained the highest proportion of votes for a 'third party' since 1923. These facts alone would guarantee June 1983 a place in the record books.

But beneath these figures the true historical comparisons are still more striking. Thatcher was elected prime minister on the lowest real proportion of the vote received by any government with a safe majority in Parliament in British history. The election revealed not only a massive decline of the Labour vote but also underlined a fall in support for the Conservative Party which has been going on for 50 years. In major areas of the British state – Scotland, the North of Ireland, the big cities – the Conservative Party received a far lower proportion of the vote than it did even in 1945, the year of its crushing defeat. Simultaneously, Labour was annihilated in large areas of the South of England. These facts are more like the symptoms of a major break-up of the political system than simply a shift from one election to the next.

The reality becomes even clearer when we look at the results in greater detail. The idea that electoral politics in Britain is about relatively uniform swings between parties disappears amid a situation where no British party had any support at all in the North of Ireland, where in Scotland the Conservative share of the vote fell to the lowest level for 115 years, and where in the South East of England the Conservatives had a 39 per cent lead over the Labour Party. The *Economist*, in its review of the results on 18 June 1983, even suggested that two separate electoral systems were appearing, with Labour fighting the Alliance in the North and the Tories fighting the Alliance in the South.

Neither were these electoral results produced by purely short-term trends. The Tory vote has been declining for 50 years, the Labour vote for 30. Support for the Liberals has been rising for three decades. The big cities have been moving against the Tories since 1959, The South East of England against Labour since 1966. The North–South divide has been deepening since 1945. Whatever is reshaping British politics it is certainly not some purely short-term process. The trends and shifts seen in the 1983 election have enormous structural roots in British society. These developments, and their motor forces, form the subject-matter of this book.

The line of approach taken here in considering modern British politics may however surprise some on the left. The book deals not with the decline of Labour but with the rise and decline of the *Conservative* Party – a decline which you would not even know was taking place from the amount of attention given to it in the press. This decline is analysed not in order to provide easy optimism for the left but, on the contrary, to point out the extreme difficulties, as well as opportunities, for socialists in the years to come. The decline in the Labour Party vote – which is every bit as serious as the press generally claims – is all the more important *because of* the huge political contradictions which are now accumulating in British society.

For the Conservative Party is not just 'another' party in British politics. It is the dominant party of the modern political system. It is the Conservative Party which has been in office for three times as long as any other party. It is the supporters and backers of the Conservative Party who control the economy and highest positions of the state. Conservative supremacy has been maintained throughout the decline and now the resurgence of the Liberal Party and the entire life of the Labour

Party. Labour was at best only ever a junior partner in a political system dominated by the Tories.

Once the development of the Conservative Party *is* understood, however, then everything else falls into place. The trends outlined – the North–South divide, the incredible assault on the Labour Party and the decline of its vote, the emergence of third parties, the huge regional differences – all form part of a coherent process within British politics. This process has been in train not for 30 , but for 137 years: *it is the post-1846 rise and decline of the Conservative Party*. Looking at it will enable us to see the shape of British politics not merely as it has developed over months or years, but over decades and even centuries.

The plan of the book is as follows. Chapters 1 and 2 look at the overall development of electoral support from the emergence of the Conservative Party in 1846 to the present. They establish that over and above all short-term trends the Conservative Party consistently increased its support up to 1931, after which a fundamental process of decline set in which is still continuing.

Chapters 3–6 outline the relationship between the Tory Party and the ruling class. They show that the Conservative Party is not a mere reflection of British capitalism but has historically organised a definite set of interests within it. At the core of the Tory Party is a great complex of firms based on foreign investment, banks, and suppliers of the internal working-class market. These are by far the most powerful sections of British capitalism and manufacturing industry based in Britain has been historically quite subordinate to their interests.

Chapters 7–9 show how this complex of capitalist interests progressively welded wider and wider layers of the population around it to create an authentically dominant political bloc. Starting from a base in the South East of England, and the English countryside, the Conservative Party progressively spread out until it brought more and more areas under its political domination. At its peak the Conservative Party reached a level of support achieved by no other party in modern British history. It acted as a great political cement with sufficient mass support in all areas and layers of society to give a tremendous solidity and stability to British politics.

Finally the book traces the economic and social processes which have undermined the Conservative bloc – necessitating the project of Thatcherism itself and the creation of the SDP–Liberal Alliance – and which fuel the crisis of the Labour Party. When this rise and decline of the Conservative Party is understood then all the fundamental features of modern British politics fall into place.

First, however, and to set all these in context, let us start by separating fact from fiction in the outcome of the 1983 election.

1.

Thatcher's Fake Landslide

In terms of seats in Parliament Thatcher's election victory of
1983 was enormous. But the Conservatives' 144-seat majority
had little to do with real degrees of popular support; it merely
reflected the grotesquely undemocratic character of the British
electoral system. The Tories won 61.1 per cent of the seats on
42.4 per cent of the vote. The Tory percentage of the vote
actually fell by 1.5 per cent from 1979 while their number of
seats increased by almost 8 per cent.

Table 1   **Percentage of votes and percentage of seats in 1983**

	Percentage of votes	Percentage of seats	Change in seats if allocated proportionally
Tories	42.4	61.1	−121
Labour	27.6	32.2	− 30
Alliance	25.4	3.5	+142
Others	4.6	3.2	+ 9

Table 1 gives the percentage of votes and seats won by the
major parties. It also shows what changes that would be
brought about by allocating seats in direct proportion to the
percentage of votes received.

The effect of the 'first past the post' electoral system is not,
contrary to the rhetoric of David Owen and David Steel, that
Labour is over-represented in Parliament because it is un-

democratically holding on to a lot of seats in the North of England. Labour's proportion of seats in 1983 was slightly, but not
massively, above its proportion of the vote. The party which
was absurdly over-represented in Parliament was Margaret
Thatcher's Tories. The chief effect of proportional representation in 1983 would not have been to reduce Labour representation but to have eliminated a large part of the 'hang 'em, flog
'em, lock 'em up' brigade of Tory backbenchers and replace
them with up-and-coming members of the SDP–Liberal
Alliance.

The decline of the Tory vote

Real political and social trends, and underlying strength, cannot be judged from one election alone, however. A 1.5 per
cent fall in the vote for the Tory Party on the face of it looks
quite a good result given that no government since 1959 has
been re-elected after a full term. Its significance only becomes
clear when it is seen in the context of the long-term decline of
Conservative Party support. Figure 1 illustrates the percentage
of the vote gained by the Conservative Party in every election
since its highest-ever level of 1931. An even longer-term curve
of Tory support, to show that we have not 'cooked the books'
by adopting an arbitrary starting-point, can be found in
Chapter 2.

What Figure 1 shows, as one would expect, is a whole series of short-term fluctuations of Tory support from election to
election, and from victories to defeats. But all these short-
term shifts are simply superimposed on a quite clear continuing decline of Tory support. With the exception of 1945–51,
when the Conservative vote was temporarily depressed by the
colossal post-war Labour landslide, every Conservative victory since 1931 has seen the Tory vote at a lower level than
the one before. Each consecutive Tory defeat saw the Conservative vote fall to a lower figure than the one previously
(see Table 2).

In the 1983 election Thatcher has not succeeded in reversing
this long-term trend of Tory decline. On the contrary her votes

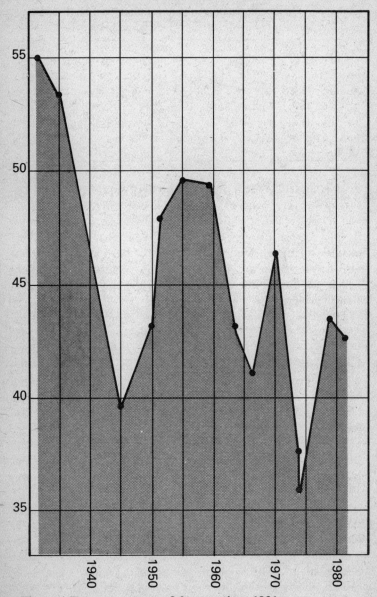

Figure 1 **Tory percentage of the vote since 1931**

Table 2   **Tory performance in general elections, 1931–83**

Tory victories		Tory defeats	
Year	Tory % of the vote	Year	Tory % of the vote
1931	55.0	1945	39.6
1935	53.3	1950	43.4
1951	48.0	1964	43.4
1955	49.7	1966	41.9
1959	49.4	1974 (Feb)	37.9
1970	46.4	1974 (Oct)	35.8
1979	43.9		
1983	42.4		

in 1979 and 1983 form *part* of that fall of support for the Conservative Party. Furthermore this Conservative decline, as we will see later, is not some sort of curious statistical freak but is deeply rooted in long-term social forces. The 1979 and 1983 elections demonstrated the weakness of the Labour Party but also a *failure* by the Tories to regain popularity – a failure which has profound consequences for the shape and future of British politics.

Three-party politics

Finally, Table 3 shows the decline of the Tory vote in the overall development of the party system. It clearly shows the way in which support for all three major parties in the 1983 election forms a coherent part of their long-term development.

Taking the Alliance first it can be seen from Table 3 that the Liberal vote has been rising since 1955. Taking just the successive peaks the trend is from 3 per cent in 1955, to 6 per cent in 1959, 11 per cent in 1964, 19 per cent in February 1974 and 25 per cent for the SDP–Liberal Alliance in 1983. The Alliance vote is not a six-day wonder but a product of that 30-year trend of rising Liberal support.

Equally, the Labour Party vote also shows a perfectly clear development. The highest percentage Labour vote ever recorded in a general election was 48.8 per cent in 1951 – although the 48.0 per cent of 1966 was only marginally lower.

Table 3 **Percentage votes for political parties in Britain since 1951**

	Tory	Labour	Liberal/SDP[1]	Plaid Cymru/SNP[2]	Other[3]
1951	48	49	3	0	0
1955	50	46	3	0	1
1959	49	44	6	1	0
1964	43	44	11	1	1
1966	42	48	9	1	0
1970	46	43	8	2	1
1974 (Feb)	38	37	19	3	3
1974 (Oct)	36	39	18	4	3
1979	44	37	14	2	3
1983	42	28	25	2	2

1. Social Democratic Party
2. Scottish National Party
3. Chiefly votes in the North of England

If we look at the findings of Gallup polls, which have been taken since 1939, Labour's highest-ever levels of support were 52.5 per cent in January 1946 and an all-time peak of 53.5 per cent in May 1966. It was after the announcement of the introduction of incomes policy in June 1966 that Labour Party support started the remorseless downward trend from which it has never recovered. The Labour vote of June 1983 is evidently a continuation of that decline.

Taking these trends together then, it can be seen that the votes of *none* of the major political parties in the 1983 election were determined simply by short-term elements of the situation. The support of all the parties represents parts of coherent long-term trends in British politics. Ripping simply one feature out of the situation – normally, for propaganda purposes, the decline of the Labour Party vote – obscures what is taking place. In reality an enormous political process is under way affecting the position of *all* political parties in which the development of each individual party interlocks with that of the others.

2.

The Modern Party System

The reality that in the 1983 election we are considering only one link of a far longer and more fundamental political process becomes still clearer if we now take a longer time-scale than the one we have so far considered. Most modern British political analysis commences at the Second World War. However, post-war trends form only a small, if coherent, part of the 130-year development which in its totality forms the modern British party system. If we want to see clearly the whole development of this system, and the place of each party within it, then we must not start not with the post-war period but with the origins of this entire process.

The reality of this long-term party development becomes clearer if it is recalled that the two modern British capitalist parties – the Conservatives and the Liberals – were not formed separately. Both were the product of one single great political crisis – the 1846 split in the old Tory Party between Robert Peel and forces organised by Benjamin Disraeli (see Chapter 7 below). The Conservatives and Liberals are simply, so to speak, the two sides of the coin of the original crisis – the Conservatives constituting directly the continuity of the majority of the Tory Party and the Liberals being formed through the fusion of the 'Peelites' with the old Whig Party. *Both* parties came to be led by the two components of the original Tory split – Disraeli giving political coherence and leadership to the Conservatives and Peel's old lieutenant, Gladstone, becoming the great formative leader of the Liberal Party. The Labour Party, as we will see, was a later development emerging directly as a consequence of the great crisis of the Liberal Party which became acute in the 1880s and reached its head in 1886 with the split between Gladstone and Joseph Chamberlain over Irish Home Rule.

The Tory Party

If we take first the Conservatives then Figure 2 shows the proportion of the votes won by the Tory Party in every election since 1859 – the year generally taken as marking the fusion of the 'Liberal–Conservative' supporters of Peel with the Whigs to form the Liberal Party.

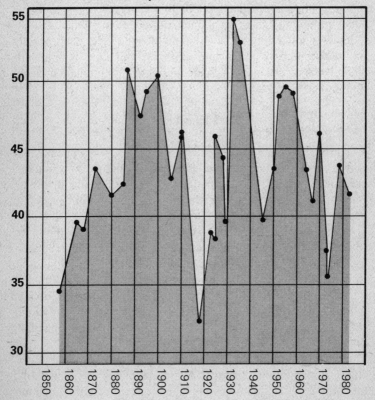

Figure 2   **Tory percentage of the popular vote, 1859–1983**

The fundamental curve of Conservative support is clear. Despite changes in the franchise, and inevitable short-term fluctuations, the Tory percentage of the vote rose remorselessly through all short-term shifts to reach a peak in 1931. Each peak of its support progressively moved higher than the one before in a cumulative chain – an equivalent graph for seats would show the Tory position rising in a similar way from immediately after the creation of the modern Conservative Party in 1846. From 1931, the trend of Conservative support relentlessly falls. Each peak is lower than the preceding one, and the successive declines see the Tory vote falling to lower levels. The 50-year fall of the Tory vote we saw in Chapter 1 is simply the descending part of this 130-year curve of Tory development. All short-term fluctuations due to political crises, specific events, changes in the right to vote, etc., are merely superimposed on that 80-year curve of rising support followed by 50 years of decline. It is scarcely possible to imagine a more clear-cut development.

The Liberal Party

The Liberal Party's development represents, so to speak, the mirror-image of that of the Conservatives. Figure 3 shows the percentage of the vote gained by the Liberal Party in every general election since 1859 – the 1983 figures, of course, being those for the SDP–Liberal Alliance.

Once more it can be seen that despite all changes in the right to vote, and all short-term shifts, support for the Liberal Party follows a perfectly clear trend of development. For 92 years – from its creation in 1859 up to 1951 – support for the Liberal Party declined. Old British Liberalism was, so to speak, dying before it was born. The Liberal Party received its highest-ever share of the vote in the year of its creation – 1859. After that the story was downhill for almost a century.

It is worth noting that within this decline 1886 represented a clear turning-point. From 1859 to 1885 the Liberal Party defeated the Conservatives in the vote in six general elections out of six – in fact, the Tories were defeated in the vote by the

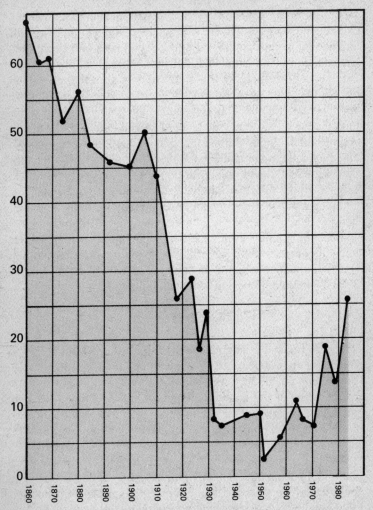

Figure 3 **Liberal Party percentage of the vote, 1859–1983**

Liberals or their predecessors the Whigs in twelve out of the thirteen general elections between 1832 and 1885. From 1886 onwards, in contrast, the Tories beat the Liberals in the vote in twenty-five general elections out of twenty-six – the sole exception being 1906. In short, the split of the Liberal Party over Irish Home Rule in 1886 altered the entire historical balance between the Liberal and Tory Parties and represents one of the great earthquakes of British political history.

Finally, from these figures it can also be seen that there was no 'Strange Death of Liberal England' during or just before the First World War – as George Dangerfield suggested in his famous book of that title. The Liberal Party had been in decline for 57 years *before* the split of 1916 between Asquith and Lloyd George. The First World War was merely the kick that knocked down the entire rotting structure of the old Liberal Party. The famous period of Liberal government of 1906–15 was the dying spasm of an already mortally wounded beast.

After 1951 a new cycle of Liberal development began. After 92 years of decline the Liberal Party vote turned upwards and has continued to rise for 32 years. The Liberal–SDP vote of 1983 is just a continuation of that trend.

The Labour Party

The beneficiary of the great crisis of the Liberals after 1886 was of course the Labour Party. However, it is not true, as is some-times claimed, that the rise of the Labour Party was *the cause* of the crisis of the Liberals. The Liberal Party was already in profound decline *before* the Labour Party ever came into exis-tence. The backbone of the Liberal Party was already smashed in 1886 – 14 years before the Labour Party was formed.

What is evident, however, is that the same processes that were destroying Liberalism also created the Labour Party. In essence, as we shall see, the Labour Party replaced the Liber-als in their chief social and geographical areas of strength.

Finally the politics of the Labour Party also grew up in the shadow of the Liberals. Those who laugh at Lenin's famous description of Labour as a 'Liberal–Labour Party' should in reality take it a little more literally at least as far as Labour's high-level practical policies are concerned. In 1900 the first act of the leadership of the new Labour Party was to enter into a secret electoral agreement with the Liberal Party. The last major act of what may transpire to have been the last majority Labour government of the old style – the 1974–79 Wilson/Callaghan administration – was to enter into a parliamentary pact with the Liberal Party. The great gods of post-war Labour policy – William Beveridge and John Maynard Keynes – were both to become Liberals. The split from Labour, both of personnel and votes, to form the SDP went on to form a bloc with the Liberals.

In its political and social base, the Labour Party had in a sense always contained two rather different components. One was the element of a mass independent working-class and at least vaguely socialist party. The other was the residue of the old Liberal Party when the latter was no longer a viable political instrument. Subject that combination to a major crisis and it would inevitably tend to dissolve into its constituent parts – precisely as happened in 1981 with the SDP split.

Figure 4 gives the percentage of the vote for the Labour Party in every general election since its foundation in 1900. (See next page.)

With inevitable short-term fluctuations Labour Party support rose progressively from the foundation of the party in 1900 until 1951. There was then no fundamental decline between the two peak Labour votes of 48.8 per cent in 1951 and 48.0 per cent in 1966, but *after* 1966 the move of the Labour vote is remorselessly downwards.

As with the Tories and Liberals, any serious study of the Labour Party must account not merely for short-term shifts, but also for that long curve of development.

Summary

Finally, to summarise these developments, it is clear that the chief trends of the 1983 election were in no real sense determined by short-term factors. All the events to which the press gives such importance – the personality of the leaders, particular manifestos, great 'crises' – had very little to do with its chief features. These explain perhaps fluctuations of a few per cent

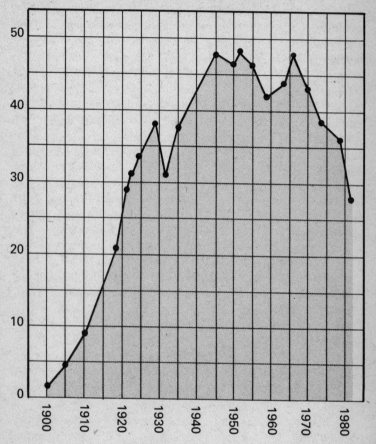

Figure 4 **Labour Party percentage of the vote, 1900–83**

in either direction. But they cannot even remotely explain the enormous historical curves of support, operating over a 137-year period, which we have looked at and of which the 1983 election is a coherent part.

The Conservative Party, as we have seen, has a perfectly clear path of development. The modern Conservative Party was formed as the majority of the split of the old Tory Party in 1846. The Conservative Party's support rose, through inevitable short-term fluctuations, for 80 years up to 1931. It achieved a position as the pre-eminent capitalist party through the split of the Liberal Party in 1886. Its support has progressively declined since 1931 and Margaret Thatcher, oil revenues, Falklands factors, hysterical press campaigns, etc., have proved quite unable to halt that underlying decline – nor would we of course expect such superficial elements of the situation to reverse a process which has been going on for over 130 years. This Tory development in turn forms part of an immense party political system which has been in existence as long as the Conservative Party itself.

What then is the nature of this Conservative Party, its 137-year development, and the party political system of which it is such an integral part? This forms the subject of the rest of the book.

3.

The Tory Elite

Any analysis of the Tory Party itself might as well start at the top. A suitable point of departure is the original membership of Thatcher's 1979 Cabinet.

The team that launched the Thatcherite project was in fact fairly typical of Conservative Cabinets. Of its members, 71 per cent were company directors, 14 per cent were large landowners, and 10 per cent were lawyers – with some overlap between the categories of landowner and company director. Eighty-six per cent of the Cabinet had been to public school. Only one out of 22 was a woman (increased to two after the Cabinet reshuffle of September 1981, but reduced to one again in 1983).

Moving down a rung to look at Tory MPs in the original Thatcherite Parliament we find that 170 (50.1 per cent) were directors of companies – in fact between them these 170 were on the boards of 475 private companies. (The equivalent figures for Labour MPs were 0.6 per cent on the boards of three private companies – and a further 0.6 per cent on the 'boards' of co-operative societies.)

If we take the principal occupations, as opposed to simply the membership of company boards, an identical pattern shows up. Of Tory MPs 40.6 per cent had direct business backgrounds as executives, managers, bankers, stockbrokers, or farmers.

The 'professional' layers which made up virtually all the rest of Tory MPs also had a very definite character. By far the largest number of these were lawyers and accountants – making up 24.1 per cent of all Tory MPs. Of the rest, 5.8 per cent came from the armed forces and 2.4 per cent from the apparatus of the Tory Party or employers' organisations. Taken as a whole, 73.0 per cent of Tory MPs were products of public schools – 14.7 per cent from Eton alone.

In other words, the Tory Party in Parliament and government is totally dominated by company boards, professions closely tied to business such as accountancy and law, and some sections of the state apparatus such as the armed forces. These, together with the apparatus of the Tory Party and employers' organisations themselves, made up 73 per cent of Tory MPs. All other groups pale into insignificance compared with these layers.

The party outside Parliament

The Tory Party leadership locally, as one would expect, is less narrowly recruited. But it still shows an identical basic shape. A survey for 1969 showed 33 per cent of constituency chairpersons of Conservative Associations to be owners of large or medium businesses, company directors, or executives. A further 16 per cent were small businessmen/women and 9 per cent were farmers or landowners. (i.e. 58 per cent of Conservative constituency chairpersons came directly from business or management occupations). A further 14 per cent were lawyers or accountants.

The situation is similar among the wider membership of the Conservative Party. A 1964 survey indicated that 40 per cent of Conservative Party members and 42 per cent of Conservative activists (and 85 per cent of constituency chairpersons) were made up of employers, managers, and 'higher professional' layers.

Educationally the only major difference between Conservatives in Parliament and senior layers outside was a distinction between constituency chairpersons in Conservative-held seats and those in Labour-held ones. In safe Conservative seats 52 per cent of constituency chairpersons came from public schools and in Tory marginals, 44 per cent. In marginal Labour seats, however, only 25 per cent of Conservative constituency chairpersons were educated at public schools and in safe Labour seats only 20 per cent were.

In other words, at the local level, the same backbone of business and business-oriented professions, educated in public schools, dominated the Tory heartland. The Tory Party was slightly more ragged round the edges in Labour areas.

Labour and Conservatives

It is also worth comparing these figures to those for the Labour Party because there has been some confused discussion in recent years about a 'convergence' between the social origins and occupations of Labour and Tory MPs. Quite apart from the much more fundamental issue of the social nature and financing of the two parties this argument is simply not factually true and can only be sustained by sloppy use of journalistic formulas such as 'middle class' and 'professional'. Table 4 shows the main occupations from which Labour and Tory MPs came in 1979 and also compares their educational backgrounds and company directorships.

Table 4 **Chief occupations of Tory and Labour MPs elected in 1979**

	Tory (%)	Labour (%)
Business (managers, bankers, stockbrokers, farmers)	40.6	5.0
Lawyers and accountants	24.1	10.8
Journalists and broadcasters	9.1	4.8
Armed services	5.8	—
Teachers and lecturers	5.3	20.8
Civil service and local government	4.1	7.4
Political, employers' and trade union organisations	2.4	4.8
Clerical and manual workers	2.2	37.2
Other	6.4	9.2
Company directors	50.1	0.6
Public school	73.0	17.0

It can be seen from this Table that it is quite simply misleading, and obscures the fundamental features, to talk of Labour and Tory MPs becoming increasingly 'middle class'.

This is not, of course, intended to justify the existing social composition of MPs. There *is* a stupendous lack of social representativeness in the MPs of both parties. Manual workers are essentially non-existent among Tory MPs and only around a sixth of Labour ones – most of those in the category of 'manual and clerical workers' had in fact ceased to work at these jobs many years before. The percentage of women Labour MPs and candidates in 1979 cannot be considered any more creditable than that of the Conservative Party (5 per cent to 2 per cent in favour of Labour among women MPs, and 8 per cent to 5 per cent among candidates). There were only two black Tory candidates in 1979 and only one black Labour candidate. Only one more woman was elected to Parliament in 1983 than in 1979.

But taking the social layers which *are* represented, these are evidently *not* the same for Labour MPs and Tory MPs. The Labour MPs represent essentially layers based in the organisations of the labour movement and parts of the public sector such as education, local government, and the civil service. These make up 70 per cent of Labour MPs. The equivalent occupations to these made up only 14 per cent of Tory MPs. Tory professionals are not drawn from occupations such as the state education system but from the traditional occupations of private enterprise such as law and accountancy.

Whatever Tory and Labour MPs represent, therefore, the social layers they come from are evidently *not* the same. We will consider later whether the top personnel of the Tory Party actually correspond to the overall character of the party.

International comparisons

Finally it is worth comparing the Tory Party with the capitalist parties of other major countries.

Taking first the United States, the US legislature is much more dominated by corporation and other lawyers than the British one. In 1982, for example, 57 per cent of the US Senate was made up of lawyers – compared to 21 per cent of Tory MPs and 9 per cent of Labour MPs. There is also in the United States the famous 'fringe' of astronauts, actors, 'machine politicians', etc.

The most serious business of government in the United States, and also the most direct input of the capitalist corporations in terms of personnel, is the role of professionals financed by major companies on bodies which are wholly unelected. Typical examples are Reagan's Secretary of Defense Caspar Weinberger and Secretary of State George Schulz, who were both top officials of the Bechtel Corporation – which is the largest overseas construction contractor in the world. Other typical figures of the same type were, or are: Dean Rusk (president of the Rockefeller Foundation and Secretary of State); Dean Acheson (corporation lawyer and Secretary of State); Robert McNamara (successively president of Ford's, Kennedy's Secretary for Defense, and then head of the World Bank) and Henry Kissinger (writer of *Nuclear Weapons and Foreign Policy*, worker for the Council on Foreign Relations, and then Nixon's National Security Adviser and Secretary of State). The formal separation of legislature and executive in the American system means that such figures need not run for office, but are appointed by the President.

The business connections of the British Tory Cabinets, as we have seen, are as impeccable as their US counterparts – indeed, they are probably much more directly involved in the ownership of capital than many of those listed above for the United States. But the Tories are also not merely members of the Cabinet but also members of the legislature – a privilege denied to their American counterparts. The direct connection between the economic organisation of the capitalist class and the exercise of power is, if anything, even greater in the Tory Party than in the political parties of the United States.

The comparison with the major capitalist parties of Western Europe is also striking. To take just one example, the Christian Democratic Union/Christian Social Union, which is the dominant party of West German capitalism, attempts to give a much greater image of democracy and social representativeness than does the Tory Party. In 1969 56 per cent of CDU/ CSU members of parliament were teachers, civil servants, trade union officials, party full-timers, and local politicians – compared with 73 per cent of Tory MPs who were company directors, managers, lawyers, accountants, members of the armed forces, or members of employers' organisations. This difference was sharply highlighted when the West German and Italian Christian Democrats refused to work in a common group with the Tories in the European Parliament. The reason they gave was that they were 'people's' parties not 'Conservative' parties and presented themselves as much more representative than the Tory Party.

The personnel of the Conservative Party, in short, are thoroughly, and indeed one might say extravagantly, capitalist in character. The connection of the Tory Party and the ruling class is one of the closest and tightest of any capitalist party in the world.

4.

Aristocrats and Others

Turning from the immediate personnel of the Tory Party to its more long-term development, there is another feature which authentically marks off the Conservatives from the capitalist parties of almost any other major country. This is the degree to which ultra-archaic social layers have survived within the Tory Party in particular and the British ruling class in general. Furthermore, while these features sometimes appear merely absurd, in reality they reflect extremely profound aspects of the nature and structure of British capitalism and its chief political party.

The aristocracy and gentry

Taking the most archaic layers of British society, the aristocracy and landed gentry, the prolonged influence, and earlier the total dominance, of these forces in British politics is quite extraordinary.

The Parliament of 1841–47, during which the modern Conservative Party was created, first met 9 years after the Parliamentary Reform Act of 1832 and 70 years after the date generally taken as the beginning of the Industrial Revolution. In this House of Commons, however, 81 per cent of MPs still came from the families of the aristocracy and landed gentry. Taking a slightly later period the radical barrister Bernard Cracroft showed, in a famous article published on the eve of the second Reform Act, that 326 out of 658 MPs (i.e. 50 per cent) in 1865 were directly members of aristocratic or titled

families. A further 170 represented directly landed or territor-
ial interests. In other words, a full three-quarters of the House
of Commons was, at this time, still made up of representatives
of landowners.

At the higher levels of government the situation was still
more extreme. Palmerston's Cabinet of 1865 was made up of
two dukes, one elder son of a duke, six lords, two baronets,
one son of a peer, one son of a baronet, and only two persons
who were not related directly to titled families. Gladstone's
Cabinet of 1880 still contained a majority of aristocrats – those
involved being a duke, a marquess, and five earls. Gladstone
himself was the son of a baronet.

In 1909 members of aristocratic families still made up 16 per
cent of the House of Commons and non-aristocratic landowners a further 15 per cent (i.e. 31 per cent in all). Furthermore, unlike the situation in other countries, this figure did not
drop after the First World War. In Germany, on the other
hand, the number of those descended from aristocratic families
elected to the Reichstag fell from 14 per cent in 1912 to 4 per
cent in 1930. The 16 per cent of British MPs who came from
aristocratic families in 1909 had only dropped to 15 per cent by
1928. In 1920 the Duke of Devonshire alone had sixteen relatives in the House of Commons.

Finally, even if we take the aristocracy in the most restricted
sense – that is sons or daughters of hereditary peers excluding
all nephews, nieces, cousins, relatives by marriage, etc. – then
these still constituted 8.5 per cent of Tory MPs in 1924 (this
had fallen to 3.2 per cent by 1974). Taking people who had or
would inherit hereditary titles, they declined from 24 per cent
of the House of Commons in 1832, to 21 per cent in 1868, 16
per cent in 1885, 16 per cent in 1900, and 13 per cent in 1918.

Cabinet and government

At the highest levels of government the prevalence of aristocratic and landowning families declined even more slowly. Prior
to the First World War, no British Cabinet contained less than
35 per cent of members of aristocratic families. Thereafter, the

numbers began to drop rapidly for all parties other than the Conservatives. Only three out of twenty-one members (14 per cent) of Lloyd George's Cabinet of 1916 were from aristocratic families. The figures were then 16 per cent in the MacDonald Labour government of 1923, 11 per cent in the 1929 Labour government, 0 per cent of the 1945 Attlee government, and an average of 5 per cent in Labour governments after that.

In the Tory Party, by contrast, the role of members directly associated with aristocratic families continued far longer and no equivalent fall occurred during or after the First World War. Members of aristocratic families constituted 47 per cent of the Balfour Tory Cabinet in 1902, 43 per cent of the Baldwin Cabinet of 1935, and 31 per cent of the Churchill Cabinet of 1951. The fall was then to 28 per cent in the Eden Cabinet of 1955, 22 per cent in the Macmillan Cabinet of 1957, 21 per cent in the Home Cabinet of 1963, and 22 per cent in the Heath Cabinet of 1970.

If a wider circle than the Cabinet is taken, and other sections of the ruling class are also considered, then the continuation of ultra-archaic features in the British ruling class may be seen simply by considering two central aristocratic families – those of the Dukes of Marlborough and the Dukes of Devonshire. As late as 1960 these two families together included in their membership, by direct descent and by marriage, nine senior Conservative ministers (the prime minister, the foreign secretary, the secretary for war, the minister for agriculture, the minister for commonwealth relations, the minister for labour, the minister for works, the minister for power, and the attorney general); two junior ministers (the under-secretary at the Foreign Office, the under-secretary for commonwealth relations); five members of the boards or owners of four newspapers (the *Times*, the *Daily Mail*, the *Daily Express*, and the *Observer*); the governor and deputy-governor of the Bank of England; six directors of three merchant banks (Hambros, Lazards, Morgan Grenfell); three directors of the Guinness brewery firm; a director of the Courtauld's textile firm; the ambassador to the United States; and the governor-general of New Zealand. The prime minister (Macmillan) was related through his marriage in the

Devonshire family to the president of the United States (Kennedy) and the Marlboroughs contained the supreme icon of the Tory Party, Sir Winston Churchill. Finally, it is worth noting that both families at an earlier period were united through the person of the Duke of Abercorn and therefore, more distantly, *all* the above were related to each other.

The last aristocrat to be British prime minister was Sir Alec Douglas Home in 1964. His predecessor was Harold Macmillan – whose Devonshire connections I've just outlined. His predecessor was Anthony Eden – a member of a landed family. Eden's predecessor, in turn, was the grandson of the seventh Duke of Marlborough and for 18 years heir to the title – Sir Winston Churchill. No post-war Conservative prime minister failed to come from an aristocratic or landowning family until Edward Heath in 1970.

More structurally, Britain is today of course, with the House of Lords, the only major country in the world in which the hereditary peerage have a right to vote in the legislature. As late as 1893 the House of Lords was powerful enough to veto a measure as fundamental as Home Rule for Ireland – although a similar attempt to veto the budget of 1909 was defeated through a major constitutional crisis and two general elections. In 1950–51 the House of Lords could still sabotage the nationalisation of the steel industry.

Landowners

We have already noted that 81 per cent of MPs in 1847 came from landed families. They still produced 49 per cent in 1880 – when the Liberals, not the Conservatives, formed the government.

Turning to the Tory Party more specifically, a clear pattern emerges. The majority of Tory MPs remained landowners until the 1870s. Thereafter, a slow decline began with the proportion of landed families among Tory MPs falling to 46 per cent in 1885 and 39 per cent by 1900 – although even this figure is extremely high. While of course farmers cannot be precisely compared to nineteenth-century landowners, nevertheless it is interesting to note that even in 1979 farmers accounted for 12 per cent of Tory MPs. Thatcher's 1979 Cabinet still contained two members who were large landowners (Whitelaw and Carrington), and one inheritor of a seventeenth-century stately home (Pym). For some comparison we may note that 0.3 per cent of Labour MPs in 1979 were farmers.

The forces which replaced the Tory landowners from the 1880s onwards were, naturally, those coming from industry and commerce – a process which speeded up after the 1886 split of the Liberal Party. Among new Tory MPs, as opposed to sitting members, the number of landowners declined from 37 per cent in 1886 to 29 per cent in 1900 while the number from industry and commerce increased from 28 per cent to 43 per cent in the same period. Overall, however, members of landowning families *still* exceeded the number of Tory MPs from industry and commerce even in the Parliament of 1900 (by 39 per cent to 32 per cent).

Public schools

It is this pattern of development in the Conservative Party which also makes it easy to understand the significance within the party, and the British ruling class generally, of that supremely English institution – the public school.

While the direct role of landowners and aristocrats has declined in the Tory Party in the twentieth century – even if not as rapidly as is generally supposed – the weight of the public schools has not diminished significantly. As we will return to this later we will deal here only with the most essential points.

It has often been said, entirely correctly, that the public schools, in their present form, were the essential institutions created by the ruling class in the nineteenth century to achieve the cultural homogenisation of the capitalist class through a common education of its children. Thomas Arnold was appointed headmaster of Rugby school in 1828 and set about converting institutions which previously had been chiefly famous for dissolute behaviour into serious educational institutions. This task was then consolidated and codified through the official government Clarendon Commission of 1861–64.

The basis on which this homogenisation was to be created, however, was unequivocally clear. The public schools were to embody a cultural supremacy of the values of the landed aristocracy and gentry over the rising industrial capitalist layers which had emerged in the late eighteenth and early nineteenth centuries. At its most crude level this was the famous declaration by Gladstone of the value of the 'classical education' of Latin and Greek over science and technology:

> The relation of pure science, natural science, modern languages, modern history and the rest to the old classical training, ought to be founded on a principle . . . I deny their right to a parallel or equal position; their true position is ancillary, and as ancillary it ought to be limited and restrained without scruples.

This precept was certainly put into practice. At Shrewsbury, one of the nine founding public schools investigated and 'reformed' through the Clarendon Commission, not one lesson in science was given before 1877. At Rugby, the pioneer public school, science equipment was excluded from the school premises and placed in the town hall – where it was 'locked up in two cases so that the townspeople could use the space for other purposes at night'. At Cambridge in 1872 only twelve persons were studying for the natural science examinations – and the majority of these were training to be doctors.

This educational system, and choice of subjects, might of course appear merely grotesque until it is set against its correct framework – its consequences for future economic, social and political development. To understand what the facts given above signify, it is necessary to note that by 1872 eleven technical and twenty other universities existed in Germany. In the United States, well over seventy universities existed by 1870 and the systematic organisation of postgraduate scientific education, copied from Germany, had already been introduced. At that time there were only four universities in the whole of England. There were also a further four universities in Scotland, where the education system was qualitatively superior.

This influence and effect worked itself all the way down the educational system with consequences lasting to the present day. In the late nineteenth century, when Germany was establishing universal primary education and an unparalleled system of technical and engineering education, the future Tory prime minister Lord Salisbury characterised the attempt to establish systematic primary education in Britain as 'pumping learning into louts'. By 1900 the average German worker had spent 32 hours a week for 9 years in school and then spent a further 5 hours a week for 2 to 4 years in part-time education. The average English worker, in contrast, received 2 years less in school, with only two-thirds of the hours, and with no systematic part-time education afterwards.

If you take that type of difference in education and training, multiply it by 20 million workers, and extend the process over decades, then the directly *economic* effects, let alone the educational and cultural ones, will be – and were – staggering.

Looking at higher levels of education, the situation is much the same. By 1957 Britain had the lowest proportion of university places per head of the population of any country in Europe except for Ireland, Norway and Turkey. The number of university places per head was 65 per cent higher in West Germany than in Britain, 114 per cent higher in France, 454 per cent higher in the Soviet Union, and 818 per cent higher in the United States. It was even 198 per cent higher in Argentina. The famous ignorance and philistinism of the British ruling class is not a mere quirk but has a profound institutional background. Sir Keith Joseph is today building on a Tory tradition.

No matter what happened to the rest of the education system, however, the public schools brought about a profound homogenisation of the various elements which made up the British capitalist class, and the leadership of its political parties. If we take the period from 1867 to 1916, then 32 per cent of all Cabinet members, including Liberals, were educated at a single school – Eton. Taking all public schools together, the figure was 59 per cent.

If we take simply Tory MPs and Cabinet ministers, then the supreme peak of dominance of Tory MPs by members educated in public schools was reached in 1935 and 1945. In these years 81 and 85 per cent respectively of all Tory MPs were educated at public schools. Between 1906 and 1945 together an average of 79 per cent of Tory MPs were educated at public school when the party was in opposition and 75 per cent when it was in government. From 1945 to 1979 the percentage was 73 per cent when the Tory Party was in office and 78 per cent when in opposition. (This difference is accounted for by the fact that, as with constituency chairpersons, public school-educated candidates in the post-war period tended to be even more disproportionately congregated in safe Tory seats.)

Taking the higher levels of the Tory Party, 92 per cent of all Conservative Cabinet ministers between 1925 and 1955 were educated at public school. Since then, the figures have been 94 per cent in the Macmillan Cabinet of 1957; 88 per cent in the Home Cabinet of 1964; 83 per cent in the Heath Cabinet of 1970; and 81 per cent in the Thatcher Cabinet of 1983. In 1982, 33 per cent of the Thatcher Cabinet had been educated at two schools – Eton and Winchester.

While these figures are of course absurd when judged from the point of view of the general population, they are not so when compared to the leading personnel of the capitalist class itself. In 1982 Eton and Winchester, in addition to a third of Thatcher's Cabinet, had also educated the chairpersons of all five clearing banks, the heads of the home and foreign civil services, and the head and deputy heads of the BBC. Eton by itself accounted for fifty Tory MPs.

Taking various periods since the Second World War, two-thirds of all under-secretaries in the civil service, nine-tenths of all senior army officers, two-thirds of senior air force officers, four-fifths of judges, two-thirds of bishops, three-quarters of directors of clearing banks, and 50 per cent of directors of leading industrial companies were educated at public school. The Tory MPs and Cabinets might be on a different planet from the public at large but they are superlatively well integrated into the capitalist class – not merely in terms of class position, but also in terms of education and upbringing.

5.

The Finances of Toryism

So far we have concentrated on the personnel of the Tory Party. We have outlined the direct connections of its members and leaders to the capitalist class and noted the connections which become closer and closer the more one ascends the ladder of the party. However, from a fundamental point of view this question of personnel is merely an index of the nature of the Tory Party and not of its substance. Other West European capitalist parties are able to get by on a much looser connection with the direct personnel of the capitalist class than the Tory Party. If we want to understand the Conservative Party the most basic questions are who gains from its existence and policies and who supplies the practical means, the finances, to make its entire structure possible? As one might suspect, those who pay and those who gain turn out to be the same.

A landlords' party

The finances of the original Conservative Party, and before that the 'old' Tory Party, show exactly the same pattern as its membership in Parliament – confirming from another angle the character of the party. While no systematic accounts exist for Tory funds for the nineteenth century, nevertheless the situation is clear both from what partial records do exist and from elections themselves. Central Tory Party funds, as opposed to a simple reliance on local patronage, came into being some time before 1830 and had a regular existence after this date. Thus, in 1831 we find the Duke of Buccleuch contributing

£220,000 to the Tory Party (for convenience, and to allow comparisons for periods with different prices, all figures in this section have been converted into 1980 prices). Buccleuch was one of the sixteen largest landowners in Britain. Tory aristocrats Bute, Ellenborough and Powis contributed a further £88,000 at the same time. In 1857 twelve Tory peers alone donated £196,000. For the general election of 1880 Tory peers subscribed a known sum of £524,000. However, it must be remembered that this is only a fraction of the total donations and of the far higher local expenditure paid for by the Tory landowners. In short, it is quite clear that in this period up to the 1880s the Tory Party was not merely staffed but also financed essentially by landowners (we will consider its policies later).

After 1880

More recently, as we have already noted, the Tory landowners began to be complemented by substantial forces from other sections of the capitalist class. An identical shift may be found in the finances. The essential method of Tory funding used in the late nineteenth and early twentieth centuries was massive corruption in the form of the buying and selling of hereditary titles to newly rising sections of the ruling class. This of course was also a supplementary means of integration of these layers into the old Tory-dominated landowning strata.

This mechanism was simple and may be illustrated by a classic example. For the election campaign of 1900 the American businessman turned British citizen William Astor donated £20,000 to Conservative funds (a sum equivalent to £575,000 in 1980 prices). The next time the Tories were in office after this administration, that is in 1916, Astor received a peerage. He then 'spontaneously' donated £200,000 (over £2 million in 1980 prices) to the Conservative Party. By 1914 the Conservative Party had accumulated a reserve of £800,000 (£20 million in 1980 prices) essentially through promises of future creation of peerages.

The Liberal Party used similar methods to secure its finances. Between 1900 and 1906 eight people alone – Wills,

Whitley, Lever, Ashton, Langman, Horniman, Joicey, and Robinson – donated £130,000 to the Liberal Party (£3.6 million in 1980 prices). They received in return five peerages and four baronetcies – Lever receiving both. Lloyd George, during his coalition government, built up a personal fund from the sale of titles which, with the accumulated interest and profit, allowed him to spend a minimum of £1.3 million (well over £19 million in 1980 prices) on political activities in the inter-war period.

The entire structure of party finance and bribery was furthermore tightly bound into the state and also utilised in relation to Labour Party politicians. The chief technical organiser of the system – a failed actor and suspected murderer named Maundy Gregory – was provided in the 1930s with a secret pension to live in Paris by the ex-Conservative Party chairman John Davidson. The condition was that Gregory kept his mouth shut. To ensure that this was done the diplomatic service was almost certainly used to survey Gregory's exile. The person who donated the funds for Gregory's pension, with a contribution worth over £400,000 in 1980 prices, was duly rewarded with a baronetcy by the 1931 national government of Ramsay MacDonald and Baldwin.

Large-scale donation of money along similar lines was not confined to the Tory and Liberal Parties either – although it was concentrated there. Ramsay MacDonald, after taking over as prime minister in 1924, received a settlement for life of the interest on £40,000 (£560,000 in 1980 prices) from the manufacturer Sir Alexander Grant. Grant subsequently received a baronetcy during MacDonald's premiership. MacDonald, acting on information given by Baldwin, also appears to have believed that the Labour leaders Clynes and Henderson were involved in the Maundy Gregory scandals.

Companies and the state

In addition to organising the cover up of its earlier sources of funds, the inter-war period was used by the Tory Party to rationalise its finances and place them on a recognisably modern footing.

The person who supervised this process, John (later Lord) Davidson, is worth a mention all to himself. Before becoming Conservative Party chairman in 1927, Davidson had been private secretary to Tory Party leaders Bonar Law and Baldwin. He had also been chief civil commissioner in Baldwin's government of 1924. In this capacity Davidson had been responsible, jointly with the military and the civil service, for drawing up the secret plans to defeat the 1926 General Strike. Earlier Davidson had also been involved in the sensational release of the still mysterious 'Zinoviev letter' used to smear the Labour Party in the run up to the 1924 general election – and as late as 1956 Davidson intervened to prevent publication of an account of the role of Conservative Central Office in this affair.

The person whom Davidson recruited to be head of Conservative Party publicity, and later to establish the Conservative Research Department, was a serving army officer and member of MI5, Major Joseph Ball. Whether or not Ball actually resigned from the intelligence service when he took up the new job is, of course, a matter on which one can come to no definite conclusion. But John Ramsden, who researched the period and from whom the above details are taken, considered it probable that Ball continued to work for MI5 'during the whole time he was at Central Office'. Whatever the background of Ball and Davidson, however, Tory election expenditure on central propaganda in this inter-war period was in real terms among the highest in history. Conservative central publicity alone in 1935 was around £5 million in 1980 prices – in addition to all the local expenditure. The next highest figure for central publicity was that preceding the 1964 election.

The most essential structural innovation which Davidson introduced was to replace the funding of the Tory Party from rich individuals with direct financing from companies. The type of individual contributions indicated previously declined to the point where, by the 1970s, only 15–20 per cent of central Tory Party funds was coming from individual donations. Of the rest, approximately 60 per cent came directly from companies and around 20 per cent, with the proportion declining, from Conservative constituency parties.

Modern Tory financing

Company contributions today make up by far the largest sector
of central Tory funds: many of them 'laundered' through various intermediate bodies. The Labour Research Department,
to whose research in this field anyone who studies the subject
is enormously indebted, found that around two-thirds of traced
political contributions by companies go directly to the Conservative Party and the rest are channelled indirectly through
organisations such as British United Industrialists, the Economic League, Regional Industrial Councils, or given to bodies
such as Sir Keith Joseph's Centre for Policy Studies. However,
the sums of money involved are so large that they cannot be
successfully hidden and the picture is the same whether direct
or indirect contributions are taken. We will look at both.

Big capital

The first feature which shows up in Conservative Party funding
is that the central apparatus of the Tory Party is an organisation quite specifically financed by the very largest concentrations of British capital. Constituency contributions make up
only a small and decreasing proportion of Tory Party central
funds – 17 per cent in 1979–80 compared to 29 per cent in
1969–70. Furthermore, this figure for constituency contributions is exaggerated as it includes formal credits given to constituencies. These formal credits amount, on the Tory Party's
admission, to approximately one-sixth of the total. In short,
the real contributions of constituencies to Tory Party central
funds was around 14–15 per cent in 1979–80. The rest, that is
approximately 80–85 per cent, was divided between individual
contributions (of which the Conservative Party refuses to give
any specific details) and a minimum of 60 per cent of company
contributions.

If the origins of company funds are then considered, a clear
pattern shows up. Taking the largest sections of industrial capital alone, in 1967–77, 59 of the 200 largest industrial companies
donated funds to the Conservative Party, 39 of the second 200
did, 23 of the third 200 did, and 27 of the fourth 200 gave donations. In short, Conservative Party donations came differen-

tially from the largest industrial companies, with 98 out of the largest 400 donating and only 50 out of the next 400 doing so.

If a wider range of companies is taken, and the financial sector is included, then as Francine Miller and Richard Minns found in a survey in 1979, 60 per cent of large firms contributed to the Tory Party, whereas only 30 per cent of smaller firms did. The contributions of the smaller firms amounted to only 6 per cent of the total donations. The contributions of the smallest companies of all – with a market capitalisation of less than £5 million – accounted for only 1 per cent of total contributions.

Banks, oil and food

Turning to the economic sectors from which the Tory Party receives its funds an extremely clear pattern also shows up. The Tory Party *does not* receive its funds in a way that is even remotely in a one-to-one relation with the economic structure of British capitalism. On the contrary, the financing of the Conservative Party is massively weighted towards certain sectors of the economy, which give enormously more than their proportionate size in the economy. Other major economic sectors give comparatively very small sums or nothing at all. Furthermore this bias in Tory financing continues to increase, as can be seen in Table 5.

Three sectors of the British economy (finance and property companies; food, drink and tobacco firms; construction companies) have steadily been accounting for a larger and larger proportion of Conservative Party company donations. Between them these three sectors make up regularly 45–55 per cent of all company contributions to the Tory Party. Other sectors, notably engineering and general manufacturing industry, have been progressively reducing their percentage of contributions to the Tory Party.

Furthermore the figures given in Table 5 are not simply equivalent to the relative weights of these different sectors of the economy. Excluding education, health, public administration and public utilities, finance and property companies accounted for only 10 per cent of GDP in 1981, but gave 31 per cent of company donations to the Conservative Party. Food, drink and

Table 5   **Percentage of traced direct and indirect company contributions to the Tory Party**

	1976	1977	1978	1979	1980	1981	1982*
Finance and property	30	28	27	30	31	31	31
Food, drink and tobacco	12	15	14	14	15	15	12
Construction	5	6	9	8	8	10	13
Vehicles and engineering	16	16	17	14	13	10	10
Chemicals, drugs and oil	9	8	7	6	6	6	4
Electrical engineering	2	2	4	3	6	2	3
Other manufacturing	15	12	11	14	9	9	10
Miscellaneous	12	12	10	11	12	18	17
Finance, food and construction	47	49	51	52	54	56	56
Manufacturing excluding electrical engineering, food, drink and tobacco	40	36	35	34	28	25	24

* Includes company reports published prior to the 1983 election only.
Source: Calculated from *Labour Research*, 1977–83.

tobacco manufacturers only accounted for 4 per cent of GDP, but gave 15 per cent of company contributions to the Tory Party. As we will see in the next chapter, those economic sectors which do contribute most heavily to the Conservative Party today are precisely those which had come to dominate the British capitalist class by the end of the nineteenth century. Conservative Party funds do not necessarily reflect accurately the overall structure of the British economy but do very definitely reflect the historically most powerful groups within it – a fact in line with the point already made that Conservative financing comes differentially from the largest concentrations of capital.

Who gains?

The relation between economic interest, concentration of capital, and the Tory Party becomes even clearer if we now integrate these figures with the development of the British economy under Thatcherism. It is not true, as is sometimes presented, that the period since 1979 has seen some sort of generalised collapse of production in the British economy.

On the contrary, while certain sectors of the economy declined sharply others were growing very rapidly indeed. Furthermore, while in some economic sectors the fall in production was considerable, the fall in profitability was very small even at the peak of the recession. Essentially, the experience of British capital under Thatcher breaks down into three categories.

First, certain economic sectors underwent rapid growth almost throughout the recession. These were in particular five – oil, agriculture, communications, finance and electrical engineering. Although the economy as a whole contracted by 4 per cent from 1979 to 1981, oil and natural gas output increased by 20 per cent, agricultural output by 9 per cent, and income from financial services by 6 per cent. Electrical engineering did contract at the height of the recession in 1981 but this was temporary, after growth in 1979 and 1980. In 1982 electrical engineering output expanded by over 5 per cent and electrical engineering production was 6 per cent above its level in 1978.

Second, a series of sectors of the economy underwent no major decrease in output at all despite the recession. These included food, drink and tobacco manufacturing, mining and retailing.

Third, the sectors which underwent massive decline under Thatcher were general manufacturing and construction. Manufacturing production overall declined by over 15 per cent between 1979 and 1982. By the end of 1982 manufacturing output was down to the level of 1967 – 15 years earlier. The fall in construction was even greater: it decreased by almost 20 per cent between 1979 and 1982.

But while both manufacturing and construction output declined, the profit levels in construction and manufacturing were very different. In manufacturing not only output but profits too collapsed. In construction, however, profits held up relatively well and were significantly above the average for the economy as a whole. If we take the best profits calculations available – the inflation-costed accounts prepared by the Bank of England – the return on capital in contracting and construction companies in 1981 was 10.7 per cent compared to an average of 7.5 per cent for all companies outside the oil industry.

In Table 6 major commercial and industrial sectors of the economy are arranged in order of their profitability in 1981. It is very interesting and instructive to compare this with the figures on output given above and with the information on the sources of Conservative Party finances in Table 5.

Table 6 **Profitability in 1981** (inflation-accounted)

Sector	Rate of profit
Oil	15.7
Food retailing	14.4
Health and household products	13.9
Engineering contractors	13.1
Electricals	10.8
Contracting and construction	10.7
Leisure	10.4
Stores	9.3
Brewers and distillers	8.2
Chemicals	5.5
Mechanical engineering	5.3
Motors	2.2
Average all sectors excluding oil	7.5

Source: *Bank of England Quarterly Bulletin*, September 1982.

It should be noted that the category 'engineering contractors' in Table 6 is not what is referred to in general language as the 'engineering industry' (i.e. vehicles, metal goods etc.). It includes chiefly firms such as the Davy Corporation – which is the second largest overseas construction contractor in the world – and Babcock International, another supplier of industrial plant. These are among the most internationalised of all firms in the British economy. Babcock International exports over 30 per cent of its British production and carries on almost 50 per cent of its production abroad. The Davy Corporation exports nearly two-thirds of its British production, carrying on more than 50 per cent of its production abroad.

What is clear is that if the financing of the Conservative Party does not reflect accurately the shape of the British economy as a whole, it does reflect with quite astonishing accuracy the levels of profits and changes in production which took place under the first Thatcher government. Of the growth sectors of the economy under Thatcher, we noted that oil companies do not contribute directly to the Conservative Party – although they do to pro-private industry groups such as the Economic League. Profits in banks and financial institutions cannot be calculated in the same way as those above, but they are enormous. With these exceptions, however, it is obvious that while the Conservative Party's finances do not come necessarily from the largest sectors of industry in terms of output, they do come from the most profitable – and from those which have been most rapidly expanding. Those who paid were those who gained.

Developments within manufacturing

This trend becomes even clearer if the situation *within* manufacturing industry is looked at. In Table 5 it was demonstrated that the proportion of contributions from the three core sectors for Tory finance was continuing to rise. This evidently means that the funds from other sectors, including manufacturing, were decreasing, as we showed earlier. Within the manufacturing sector there is only one significant exception to this – electrical engineering. Here, there was not a reduction but an *increase* in contributions to the Tory Party, at least up to the height of the recession in 1981 – which, as we noted, was the only time when electrical engineering output was seriously affected by the slump. In 1980, when Thatcher's party was paying off the 1979 election campaign expenses, the two electrical engineering giants – GEC and Plessey – were respectively the first and fourth largest company donators to the Conservative Party and were, after Allied Breweries, the second and third largest political contributors to all right-wing organisations in that year (i.e. including British United Industrialists, the Economic League, etc.). The three traditional core sectors of Toryism plus electrical engineering accounted for more than 60 per cent of all traced company contributions to the Tory Party in this year.

At the time of her election, Thatcher also had no more openly proclaimed admirer in industry than the head of GEC, Lord Weinstock. His ardour, judged by cash payments rather than praise, seems to have temporarily abated at the height of the recession in 1981 when GEC temporarily withdrew from giving a donation to the Conservative Party.

This new attitude of the electrical engineering industry towards the Tory Party can be contrasted, for example, to the traditional position of GEC's chief rival as Britain's largest industrial firm – Imperial Chemical Industries (ICI). ICI is a firm traditionally keeping its distance from the Conservative Party. Its chairperson in the 1960s, Paul Chambers, was a frequent critic of Tory governments and one of the chief campaigners for entry into the Common Market at a time when the Conservative Party was not at all prepared to accept all the consequences of this. Under Thatcher, the distancing of the heads of ICI from the Conservative Party has gone still further with its present chairperson, John Harvey-Jones, being an open supporter of the SDP and bitterly opposed to Thatcher's war over the Falklands. Two other smaller chemical firms, Fisons and Laporte Industries, also withdrew funding from the Conservative Party – Laporte Industries publicly declaring that it was doing so because of the policies of the Thatcher government.

The connection between these changing relations to the Conservative Party and the shifts in the economy under the Thatcher government examined earlier are rather obvious. Electrical engineering firms such as GEC or Plessey are in an industry which, apart from 1981, continued to expand almost throughout the recession. They are also locked into a great complex of heavy dependency on state expenditure on armaments, power generation, telecommunications, etc., which were among those sectors of state expenditure which *were not* cut back by the Thatcher government. GEC in particular also adopted a very specific strategy for dealing with the slump – it accumulated £1,000 million of liquid funds by the beginning of 1983 and invested them at high interest rates in the money market. As Anthony Sampson put it, in his *Changing Anatomy of*

Britain, Britain's 'largest manufacturing corporation was looking more like a bank' – which is not a bad analogy for a Tory manufacturing company.

In contrast, a firm such as ICI in the chemicals sector is not tied in a similar way into the same complex of military and state spending. For this reason, and others, while electronics output continued to expand for most of the recession, chemicals was a sector significantly hit by the slump. Whereas GEC's profits maintained themselves relatively well, ICI in 1980 suffered the first loss in its history, recovered somewhat in 1981, and then suffered another big fall in profits in 1982. In 1981 GEC, in electrical engineering, was making a profit almost 75 per cent higher than ICI in chemicals despite a turnover 40 per cent smaller and a capital employed less than half as large. The shifts in financial contributions, then, reflect the shifts in the economy itself.

These figures also show that it is not serious to suggest, as is sometimes done, that the relation of companies to the Conservative Party, or a phenonemon such as Thatcherism, is simply based on 'ideology' or 'purely political' consider-ations. Naturally, there *is* a specifically political, and even ideological, element in the relations of the ruling class to the Tory Party. All sections of the ruling class, or at least the major ones, would almost always prefer a Conservative government to a Labour one. They will defend the Tory Party as a fundamental strategic instrument even when they have sharp tactical differences with it. Nevertheless, as we have shown, there is also a very clear economic dimension. Certain sections of the capitalist class have gained enor-mously from the Conservative Party in general and That-cherism in particular and continue to finance the Tory Party to a high degree. Other economic sectors have ceased to gain as much as before and are withdrawing their level of funding. Only someone who is very naive, or deliberately wants to obscure reality, can believe that these trends are 'accidents'.

However, all this poses another question. *Why* did this extraordinary collection of landowners, banks, construction firms, and food, drink and tobacco manufacturers come to dominate the Conservative Party and the British ruling class? To see this we need to go back to look at the British capitalist class itself.

6.

The British Capitalist Class

While the material in the previous two chapters shows that the Conservative Party is superlatively well integrated into the British ruling class, it also raises an obvious question. What sort of ruling class is it whose political personnel remained until the 1880s dominated by landowners? What kind of capitalist class would leave political leadership to Greek and Latin students and allow its mass education system to be on so primitive a level as inevitably to hold back its economic future? How could the 'First Industrial Nation' come to have a ruling class party dominated by bankers and brewers?

This point is important because it relates to a common misunderstanding both of the Conservative Party and of Thatcherism – one which sees *the cause* of Britain's economic and political crisis in such questions as the weight of the public schools, the supremacy of the cultural values of landowners, etc., and believes that there is something 'irrational', from the point of view of British capitalism, in Thatcher's enormous destruction of British manufacturing industry. Such views can be found expressed at a popular level in the various editions of Anthony Sampson's *Anatomy of Britain* or, at a more sophisticated level, in what is now one of the classics on the 'British crisis' – Martin Wiener's *English Culture and the Decline of the Industrial Spirit*. At a political level such concepts form a basis of some of the political appeal of the SDP and the Liberals. On such an analysis there is of course no need to question capitalism as such in Britain. All that need be done is to remove certain of its most backward features – probably in

alliance with 'modernising' sections of the capitalist class
against 'backward' layers who support Thatcher.

While we cannot deal with all the ramifications of these
issues here (but see the *Guide to Reading*) it is simple to make
a few fundamental points. We shall do so by tracing the history
of the British capitalist class itself.

Dominance within the British ruling class

To find that the Tory Party had its origins among landowners
is not surprising. At least a century before manufacturing
industry arose on a large scale in Britain the greatest concentrations of wealth and power in the country were in the capitalist landowning class. What is not so well known, however, is
that the greatest concentrations of wealth in Britain were *still*
in the hands of the capitalist landlords probably as long as a
century *after* the Industrial Revolution had taken place. There
is not the slightest doubt about this fact, either in relation to
individual or to institutional forms of capital.

Although concentrations of personal capital are notoriously
difficult to measure accurately, a relatively reliable guide, for
the period prior to the introduction of death duties, can be
gained from wealth left at death. Records of this have been
extensively studied – by Marx in the 1860s and subsequently in
much greater detail. All these studies show essentially the
same, and extremely clear, historical distributions of wealth in
Britain.

If we take as a measure of wealth those leaving £500,000 or
more on death then the numbers of owners of such capital outside land did not overtake capitalist landlords in Britain until
the 1860s. If the criterion of leaving over £1,000,000 is taken
then the shift did not take place until the 1880s (i.e. almost
exactly the same time that the shift between the dominance of
landed and non-landed capital was taking place in the Tory
Party). Even if we assume that industrialists represented a
younger generation which died later – and there are good
reasons for assuming that this was not an important element in
the situation – this still means that for almost a century after

the Industrial Revolution it was landownership which continued to represent the greatest individual concentration of economic wealth in Britain.

This specific pattern of capitalist economic development becomes even clearer if wealth is looked at not just on an individual level, but also in terms of the concentrations of capital in the different institutions and sectors of the economy. As far as industry is concerned, Raphael Samuel, in his scintillating essay 'The Workshop of the World', has shown on what extremely small units of production the Industrial Revolution and the manufacturing economy of the Victorian epoch was based. As Samuel puts it,

> In juxtaposing hand and steam-powered technologies one is speaking of a *combined* as well as an *uneven* development. In mid-Victorian times, as earlier in the nineteenth century, they represented *concurrent* phases of capitalist development, feeding on one another's achievements, endorsing one another's effects . . . The industrial revolution rested on a broad handicraft basis, which was at once a condition of its development and a restraint on its further growth.

Any idea that Britain leapt during the Industrial Revolution from the primarily agricultural based economy of the early part of the eighteenth century into a modern industrial epoch has no basis in fact. British industrialisation followed a far more long-drawn-out course than the process seen later in Germany, Russia, or today's 'Newly Industrialising Countries'. The scale of British industry in its period of industrialisation was also incomparably smaller than that of its later rivals.

The same pattern can be seen if the concentration of industrial capital, as well as the scale of individual units of production, is considered. Even by the 1880s the largest 100 industrial firms in Britain accounted for less than 10 per cent of total production – and this had only risen to around 15 per cent by 1909. Really rapid concentration of industrial capital in Britain began only after the First World War, when the share of industrial production accounted for by the largest 100 firms rose to 26 per cent by 1930, fell slightly to 23 per cent by 1948, and then rapidly moved ahead to 33 per cent in 1958, 38 per cent in 1963, and 45 per cent in 1970. However even then, as we will see, the most powerful development and concentration of capital in Britain still existed in sectors primarily *outside* heavy industry. In countries such as Germany, the United States, and Japan, the economy became dominated by industrial sectors such as steel, electronics, chemicals, and vehicle production. In Britain the economy was dominated by banking and land, and the manufacture of food, drink, and tobacco. Only in one truly modern sector, oil, did British capitalism develop an extremely strong position – and that was particularly linked to the military needs of its navy.

Concentration of land

In contrast to the situation of industry the concentration of landed capital in Britain had acquired quite staggering proportions by the last half of the nineteenth century. The most comprehensive survey of this period, the official *Return of Owners of Land* for 1873, showed that four-fifths of the land in Britain was owned by a mere 7,000 people. In certain areas of the country the situation was even more extreme. For example, in East Anglia 350 people owned 55 per cent of the agricultural land, and in Scotland the 25 largest estates alone accounted for a quarter of all land.

Seven people – the Dukes of Buccleuch, Devonshire, Northumberland, Portland and Sutherland, the Marquess of Bute and the Earl Fitzwilliam – had estates of over 100,000 acres and annual incomes of over £100,000 each (an income approximately equivalent to £2 million in rent in 1980 purchasing power). Two others – the Dukes of Norfolk and Westminster – had smaller estates but enormous incomes due to the geographical positions of their land (the Duke of Westminster, who owns much of London's Belgravia, is still today the richest individual person in Britain). A further six people – the Duke of Richmond, the Earls of Breadalbane, Fife and Seafield, Alexander Matheson and Sir James Matheson – had slightly smaller incomes but estates even larger than 100,000 acres. These fifteen persons alone can be said to have constituted the core of the British landed capitalist class.

Finally, the actual process of the building of towns, both before and after the Industrial Revolution, itself increased the wealth of landed capital. By the end of the eighteenth century, probably one-fifth of the expansion of London in the previous 200 years had been onto land owned by dukes and much of it was on leases under which the building reverted to the landowner. By 1866 out of 261 provincial towns, 69 were largely built on land owned by great landlords and 34 by gentry.

Ireland

To rent directly derived from land in Britain another element must be added to understand the wealth of the British capitalist landowning stratum – and one with the profoundest historical consequences for the Tory Party and British politics. This is the question of Ireland. As subsequent developments have greatly distorted the true historical relations between British capitalism and Ireland, it is necessary to outline them briefly.

The first point that should be noted is that even the relative sizes of the populations of Britain and Ireland which exist today are in no sense a natural development. At the beginning of the nineteenth century the population of Ireland comprised some 33 per cent of the population of the British state. By 1966 it had fallen to less than 8 per cent of the population of the states of Britain and the South of Ireland combined. In 1966 the population of England alone was ten times that of Ireland whereas in 1821 the English population had been only one and a half times the population of Ireland.

This tremendous transformation in the relative weights of populations did not come about through 'natural' increase of the English population over the Irish. It was achieved through genocidal policies of the British state which resulted in the annihilation of large sections of the Irish people and the depopulation of large areas of the country – the South of Ireland is today the only country in Western Europe which actually has a *lower* population than the same area had at the beginning of the nineteenth century. At the time of the first Irish census of 1821 the population of what is today the Southern Irish state stood at 5,086,000. By 1961 it had fallen by almost half to 2,818,000. As a comparison, the population of England from 1801 to 1961 rose from 8,538,000 to 43,350,000 and even the population of the North of Ireland expanded marginally.

The collapse in the population of the South of Ireland is explained not by any 'voluntary' factors but by the effects of famine – above all the great famine of 1846 – mass emigration forced by poverty, and the effects of a standard of living based on mass misery. Anyone who has any illusions as to the supposedly 'peaceloving' characteristics of British politics, and of its ruling class, need not even look to the barbarous policies carried out by Britain in Asia, Africa, or the Middle East. They need simply note the regime of mass annihilation and repression in Ireland – a policy which in its cumulative effects, if not its methods, stands comparison with anything achieved by Hitler. Its policy towards Ireland alone brands the British ruling class, and the Tory Party in particular, as one of the greatest groups of mass murderers in history.

The profits which this regime of extortion and massacre produced were, however, equally astronomic. By the middle of the eighteenth century £750,000 was being extracted annually in rents from Ireland to absentee landlords in England (roughly £45 million a year in 1980 prices). To give some idea of comparison it may simply be noted that at that time a 'knight' might live quite adequately on £800 a year. By the beginning of the nineteenth century, roughly 1.5 per cent of British GNP alone was accounted for by rent from Ireland – most of it available for capital accumulation in Britain.

In the nineteenth century this struggle over British rule became one of the most decisive issues not only of Irish but of British politics. And by this time the need to maintain control of the crucial shipbuilding plants of Belfast had been added to the question of English landlordism. The outcome of this struggle, the clash over Irish Home Rule and Independence, brought Britain closer to civil war than any other event in the twentieth century. The fanatical Tory attachment to the Union with Ireland, its support for armed Unionist resistance to Home Rule and for the Curragh army mutiny of 1914, the fact that after 1886 the Conservatives publicly named themselves the 'Unionist Party' – later amended to 'Conservative and Unionist Party' – cannot be understood simply as a question of romantic attachment to Empire or the 'integrity of the British state'. It was rooted historically in the profound economic interests in Ireland of British capitalism in general and of the landed capitalist class in particular.

Industry, banking and commerce

The form of derivation of its wealth by the British landlord class gave to landed capital in Britain an enormous economic flexibility. Being derived from rent rather than tied down in direct agricultural production, capital accumulated in land could potentially be utilised in other sectors of the economy. Similarly, as no skill in agricultural production was required for landownership in Britain, it was easy for wealth made in other sectors of the economy to buy its way into land. This latter path then constituted a route to both political and social respectability and created a ready fusion of landed and various other forms of capital.

Wealth made in land was invested in trade and banking, and wealth made in trade and banking was invested in land. British landed capital, at least in its greatest concentrations, never constituted a cut-off estate as did the more feudal aristocracy of Germany, France, and other European states.

Thus, for example, the two Mathesons already referred to were from families involved in Far Eastern commerce, while London bankers and merchants (such as Lloyd, Baring, Drummond and Rothschild) all bought their way into land. So also did brewers such as Barclay, Hanbury and Whitbread as well as West Indian merchants and plantation owners. Later in the nineteenth century, industrialists such as Tennant, Armstrong, Coats and Wills repeated the same process.

Developments throughout the nineteenth century also progressively opened up wider opportunities for British landed capital to participate in more general economic activities. The development of large-scale railway building from the 1840s onwards, for example, provided enormous opportunities for investment. Initially, the railway construction directly involved buying of land on estates and later created massive opportunities for portfolio investment – a type of utilisation of funds particularly suited to the rentier incomes of British landed capital. The wholesale creation of joint-stock companies in the last half of the nineteenth century opened up opportunities for investment to any section of landed capital with money available.

Despite this increasing opening for non-agricultural forms of activity for landed capital, however, for reasons discussed later, this fusion of landed capital with other sections of the ruling class was *not* achieved in anything like an even fashion. On the contrary, the unevenness of this fusion became one of the principal features of the British ruling class. Whereas in the eighteenth century the intermixture of landed, merchant, and banking capital had been achieved, no equivalent fusion took place in the nineteenth century between *industrial* capital and wealth made in land, banking, or overseas trade. The notorious division between banking and industry in Britain in reality has its origins in the very earliest periods of British capitalism.

Landed and non-landed wealth

The separation of industrial capital from other sections of the British ruling class can be easily illustrated by the most politically active section of the capitalist class – the membership of the House of Commons. The Parliament of 1841–47 that created the Conservative Party has been subjected to an extremely detailed examination by W.O.Aydelotte. We have already noted earlier that in this Parliament 81 per cent of MPs came from landed families. A further 9 per cent had made wealth in business. Between these two capitalist interests there was some important degree of overlap – 17 per cent of members of the landowning families in the House of Commons had major connections with business outside land and 40 per cent had at least some minor business connections.

But when the actual layers of overlap are considered a rather different reality is revealed. Of the fifty MPs from landed families who were regularly connected with non-agricultural capitalism, only six were manufacturers and three others were involved in railways, whereas there were eighteen bankers, nineteen merchants, a planter, a distiller and a stockbroker. In short, significant numbers among the most politically active landed capitalists in the mid-nineteenth century were involved with merchants and banking but virtually none with manufacturing industry. Landed capitalists with manufacturing interests represented under 2 per cent of the landed families represented in the House of Commons.

Throughout the rest of the nineteenth century this pattern is also clear. Manufacturing industry had in any case ceased to expand proportionately as a sector of the British economy by the middle of the nineteenth century, and this might in any case have tended to restrict the fusion of manufacturing capital with other layers of the economy. Even more importantly, however, the British economy had already begun to undergo an internal transformation to reach a structure which was very distant from one based on the core sections of heavy industry. Although the weight of non-landed capital increased throughout most of the nineteenth century, this was not due to any increase of wealth in what in other countries would have been regarded as the heart of the industrial economy.

To show this shift in the composition of the ruling class, we may once more take both criteria of individual wealth and the institutional measures of capital. Of those leaving over £1,000,000 at death, fortunes deriving from landed capital declined from around 89 per cent of the total in 1809–58 to around 36 per cent in 1880–99 – although, as can be seen, even this latter figure is still high. Textiles, the key nineteenth-century sector of British industrial capitalism, accounted, in contrast, for around 5 per cent of the total. Furthermore the proportion of fortunes made in textiles tended to decline in the latter part of the nineteenth century.

A similar trend can be seen in the metal industry. This accounted for around 10 per cent of non-landed millionaire wealth in the first part of the nineteenth century – that is, under 5 per cent of the total – and it then declined. This pattern of individual wealth is easily explained by the changing economic structure of the period which we will discuss later.

The real sustained development of non-landed wealth from the mid-nineteenth century onwards came from layers outside the core of heavy industry. The financial and banking sector consistently accounted for between 10 and 20 per cent of those leaving more than £1,000,000 at death – meaning that land and finance between them easily accounted for the majority of the greatest concentrations of individual and family wealth in Britain. From the middle of the nineteenth century onwards the food, drink and tobacco industries also accounted for around one tenth of millionaires (i.e. twice as much as the metal industry) and from 1858 onwards the distributive trades accounted for another 5 per cent.

A similar pattern of economic power shows up *within* the manufacturing sector if we consider not just individual wealth-holders but also companies. A list of the ten largest manufacturing companies for 1914, for example, shows four textile firms, three food, drink and tobacco companies, one construction supplier, and only one firm each from engineering and chemicals. The types of companies that were by this time dominating modern German and American capitalism (Siemens and AEG in electronics, IG Farben in chemicals, Krupp, Thyssen and Carnegie in metals, Rockefeller in oil) simply *were not* the dominant sections of British industry, let alone British capital. The core of heavy manufacturing industry – metal engineering, electronics, chemicals, steel – was already, by the late nineteenth century, a subordinate section of British capitalism. The peculiarities of the Tory Party we noted earlier, the weakness, and even collapse of manufacturing industry under Thatcher, are therefore not some 'out of the blue' freak, but a logical link in an historical process.

Indeed, the point can be put very simply. The fundamental question which must be answered for the British economy is not why it is 'deindustrialising', but why it ceased to develop its manufacturing industry so early in the first place. After rapidly expanding overall from roughly 1770 to 1830, the expansion of manufacturing industry as a proportion of the British economy then ended for a century – until after the defeat of the General Strike of 1926 and the onset of the depression of the 1930s. The entire flow of labour from agriculture, and the essential proportionate growth in the economy in the last two-thirds of the nineteenth century, went into what would now be regarded as the 'service' sectors of the economy – finance, retailing, transport and communications. Only much later (around 1930), and under very different circumstances, did the growth of manufacturing industry as a proportion of the economy start again – although the effects of this have been undone, during the 1970s in general and by Thatcherism in particular. It is this grinding halt to the growth of manufacturing industry as a proportion of the British economy from roughly 1830 that underlies the relatively low level of individual and company wealth in sectors such as the metal industry, textiles, etc., and helps to explain the continued weight of landed capital and the growth of sectors such as banking, retailing and food, drink and tobacco manufacture which we have looked at.

This development of the economy, however, also explains the archaic features of the Tory Party, the nature of its leadership, the weight of the public schools and so on. As the British economy was not dominated by heavy manufacturing – as were the German and US economies, for example – the need to educate an advanced industrial workforce was a low priority for the British ruling class. So also was the creation of the type of political leadership necessary to run a modern industrial state. It was not the prevalence of public schools and the cultural supremacy of landowners that created the backwardness of the industrial structure, but the backwardness of the industrial structure which created the nature of the public schools and the cultural supremacy of landowners.

The anachronistic features of the Tory Party are not aberrant but reflect the character of the British ruling class itself. The dominance of the Tory Party corresponds to, and reflects, in the victory within the ruling class of layers outside the core of manufacturing industry. But to see *why* they were victorious we must consider why the modern political party system arose in the first place.

7.

The Origins of the Conservative Party

The great crisis: 1828–46

The background to the creation of both the modern party system and the modern British economy is the Industrial Revolution itself. After an initial surge of development in the latter part of the eighteenth century, temporarily halted in the first decade of the nineteenth, British capitalism embarked upon the most powerful surge of industrialisation in its history. By 1831 the proportion of British national income accounted for by manufacturing, mining and construction had risen to approximately 34 per cent. In the same period the proportion of national income accounted for by agriculture fell to roughly 23 per cent – making Britain the first major country in history in which industry constituted a larger part of the economy than agriculture. This creation of a fundamentally industrialised economic structure inevitably confronted the British capitalist class with problems of political domination that had never been confronted by any previous ruling class in history. The modern party and political system is precisely the attempt to confront this problem.

The difficulties of constructing a suitable system of capitalist political domination under the new conditions were further complicated by the fact that the process of industrialisation unleashed not one but *two* potentially violent forces threatening the British economic and political system.

The first such force was the industrial proletariat concentrated within the British state. Between 1811 and 1831 the proportion of the paid workforce employed in manufacturing, mining, and construction in Britain rose to over 40 per cent. This, furthermore, was a working class created under the horrors of an Industrial Revolution too well known to need describing in detail here.

The second element in the situation, however, was Ireland, already discussed in part of the previous chapter. To absentee rents extorted from Ireland were added the systematic use of Irish agricultural products – grain, butter, pork and bacon – to feed the growing towns of Britain. The Catholic population of Ireland itself was increasingly forced back on a lower and lower diet – one increasingly organised around potatoes – which culminated in the famine of 1846.

The effect of this entire system of oppression, both in Britain as a whole, and Ireland in particular, was inevitably to produce sharply increasing tendencies towards a social and political explosion. Logically these reached their first qualitative peak in the most extreme case of oppression of all, Ireland, in the 1820s. In 1823 Daniel O'Connell formed the Catholic Association to campaign against the British law banning the holding of political office by Catholics – that is, a ban on the vast majority of the Irish population. In 1828 O'Connell won the County Clare parliamentary seat – confronting the then Tory government under Wellington with a choice of admitting him to the House of Commons or facing what the government feared would be an insurrection against British rule in Ireland.

The result of this Irish crisis was to fracture the governing Tory Party. The Tory leadership, around Wellington and Peel, passed the Catholic Emancipation Act in 1829, but only after violent opposition from their base. Then, amid increasing unrest on a whole series of issues, the Tory government collapsed in 1830. It was the end of an epoch in British politics. For 47 years prior to 1830 the Tory Party, or its predecessors, had been continuously in office. After 1832 the Tory Party was defeated in the popular vote in twelve out of the thirteen next general elections up to 1885. O'Connell had precipitated a revolution in British politics.

Through the breach opened up by Ireland now flowed a whole new series of political issues. After 2 years of increasing struggles the great Parliamentary Reform Act of 1832 was passed by the new Whig administration. This largely re-cemented relations within the ruling class, but did not restore order – on the contrary, it allowed new forces to come out into the open. In 1838 the first Chartist petition for universal male suffrage in Britain was presented – the first emergence in the world of a clearly working-class mass movement. In 1839 an armed working-class insurrection took place in Newport, South Wales. In 1842, amid one of the worst industrial depressions of the nineteenth century, the second Chartist petition was presented. In the same year the first embryonic political general strike in history took place. Profound new forces were emerging into politics with tremendous disintegrative potentials for the future.

Identical trends to those in Britain were also appearing in Ireland. After 1843 O'Connell was eclipsed in influence by the Young Ireland movement – commencing a process which culminated in 1848 in the first attempted Irish armed insurrection against British rule in the nineteenth century.

Finally, the background to this entire process was rising discontent throughout Europe which culminated in the 'year of revolutions' of 1848.

1846: The creation of the modern capitalist parties

Confronted with the rising discontent of the 1840s, British capitalism had only two fundamental choices. The first was simply to engage in a head-on confrontation with the rising ferment not only in Ireland but also in Britain – a policy that ran the risk at some point of culminating in exactly the type of revolutionary developments that occurred in Europe (where such a policy was carried out) in 1848, 1870 and 1918. The second option was to use the enormous reserves and newly acquired strength of British capitalism to attempt to co-opt the movements forming against it. Given that at that time Britain accounted for more than 30 per cent of world industrial pro-

duction, or half as much again as any competitor, it is no surprise that British capitalism chose the latter course. By so
doing it was also able to surmount the economic crisis which
had been accumulating in the 1840s.

The decisive steps summing up the new orientation of the
British ruling class, and laying the basis for British economic
policy for the next century, were all taken in a mere 5-year period between 1841 and 1846 – the years inaugurating also the
structure of the modern political system. Essentially, free trade
in industrial goods had been introduced by the Tory prime
minister Robert Peel immediately on taking office in 1841.
State finance was rationalised through the reintroduction of
income tax for the first time outside war. It was the completion
of these measures by the repeal of the Corn Laws in 1846
which was then the step which split the old Tory Party and
created both modern Conservative and Liberal parties.

The Corn Laws were effectively a tariff on the import of cer-
eals – allowing import of corn duty-free only when the British
price was extremely high. They therefore gave a competitive
advantage to British agriculture at the expense of its rivals
while simultaneously maintaining an artificially high price for
all food based on grain. This arrangement benefited landowners, particularly the smaller and less efficient, but cut the
living standard of the working class, and created a pressure for
higher wages, by keeping up food prices. High food prices in
turn helped feed working-class discontent and threatened
industrial profits through the demand for higher wages.

Via a crucial economic mechanism, therefore, the Corn
Laws in reality provided for the ruling class two alternative sets
of social alliances. Maintenance of the corn tariff meant an
alliance of all sections of the ruling class with small landowners
at the expense of the working class – a perfectly suitable reactionary combination if the aim was to confront and smash the
working class. A similar political system was later used by
French capitalism and by Bismarck – and its consequences in
France and Germany were exactly the same as had confronted
the British capitalist class in the 1830s (i.e. rapidly rising working-class discontent, culminating in the 1848 revolution in

France, and the rapid rise of the German Labour Movement, culminating in the revolution of 1918).

The alternative social alliance for British capital was to scrap the Corn Laws and hold down or reduce the price of food. This would create a basis for a bloc between large landowners and the industrial bourgeoisie and also for attempts to co-opt the working class. For industrialists such a cheap food policy would help keep down money wages – permitting high profit levels while avoiding working-class discontent. Large landowners would not be adversely affected as they could survive the foreign competition. Small landowners, however, would inevitably be crushed.

In reality, therefore, behind the apparent argument on a tariff, stood two completely different systems of social alliances and two totally different political perspectives. The first – that is large landowners, with small landowners and industrialists to crush the working class – might be named, after its most famous exponent, 'Bismarckianism'. The second – large landowners, with industrialists and the working class at the expense of small landowners – may be termed after what it became, Liberalism and the Liberal Party. Peel chose the latter course of sacrificing the small landowners and his lieutenant, Gladstone, went on to lead the Liberal Party. The majority of the Tory Party, however, formed around forces organised by Benjamin Disraeli, rallied to defend its small-landowner base and against Peel's course. The outcome, as we have already seen, was the creation of *both* modern capitalist parties in Britain and the surpassing of all the old party alignments. A new 130-year party political system was put in place.

The new economic orientation

At the same time as creating the basis for British political stability, however, Peel also set in train processes that were to destroy the competitiveness of British-based manufacturing industry. Indeed, this was in a sense an *inevitable* outcome of the original decision because it had been adopted precisely to *avoid* confronting the working class – in other words, to accept a lower than possible rate of exploitation and instead grant economic concessions to the working class. The period following the 1840s therefore saw the re-establishment of political stability, but also British industry beginning to fall behind its rising American and German rivals both in terms of competitiveness and in terms of technological capacity. What is more this process was hastened by new economic mechanisms put in place to supplement and maintain the original Peelite orientation.

Of these new economic mechanisms by far the most important was British overseas investment. With a decreasingly competitive manufacturing base, but with colossal economic reserves, British investment abroad from the 1870s onwards began to reach levels equivalent to investment in Britain itself – and finally overtook it. By the First World War, profits on British investment abroad amounted to around 8 per cent of British GNP and remained at approximately 4 per cent even between the First and Second World Wars. Apart from its direct effects on the economy, overseas investment also reduced the pressure for British manufacturing industry to be internationally competitive.

To show the mechanism of this we need only take the international constraints on the British economy. British capitalism, for as long as systematic figures exist, has always had a surplus on the 'service' side of the balance of payments – shipping, travel, etc. However, this surplus was historically relatively small and at the beginning of the nineteenth century was sufficient to finance only around 10 per cent of British imports of goods ('visible' imports). This 'services' surplus then rose slightly during the course of the nineteenth century, but never reached a figure of more than around 14 per cent – which left 86–90 per cent of British visible imports to be financed by other means.

Taking other possible sources then, at the beginning of the nineteenth century, income from British overseas investment amounted to only about 10 per cent of the visible import bill (i.e. services and investment income together, prior to the 1840s, were sufficient to finance only 20 per cent of British visible imports). British visible exports, and the manufacturing industry which produced most of them, therefore simply *had* to have a high degree of international competitiveness in selling its goods. A failure of competitiveness in manufacturing could not be compensated for by the service sector or by foreign investment income and, therefore, prior to the second half of the nineteenth century, would have provoked a severe balance of payments crisis, a sharp contraction of imports, and a tremendous drive to re-establish the competitiveness of the manufacturing sector. British manufacturing industry in the early nineteenth century not merely *was* but *had to be* competitive.

What occurred over time was that the return from the flow of British investment abroad became an alternative means of financing visible imports to the necessity of having an efficient and competitive manufacturing sector. As the century wore on, the proportion of visible imports which had to be financed by visible exports (i.e. primarily manufactured goods) decreased steadily from 80 per cent in the 1820s and 1830s to just under 60 per cent on the eve of the First World War.

This represented a qualitative transformation in the nature of the British economy and its conditions for equilibrium with world economy during the second half of the nineteenth century. The answer to the famous question as to why British industry became less and less competitive compared to its rivals is simply that it had less and less *necessity* to be competitive. The international balance of the British economy could be increasingly maintained by means other than a competitive manufacturing sector – it is indeed hard to think of a purer case of Lenin's model of a foreign-investment-dominated imperialism than the British economy during the latter part of the nineteenth century. With the British economy removed from international constraints imposed by the balance of payments, British manufacturing industry could and did slide further and further behind its competitors.

The shattering effect of the two world wars, the acute new crisis which set in after 1945, can be understood in the same light. With the income from foreign investment removed by the effects of war, the proportion of visible imports which now had to be financed by visible exports rose sharply to 86 per cent in the decade after the Second World War and only decreased marginally (to 84 per cent) at the end of the 1960s. British manufacturing industry simply had to become competitive again – with the entire crisis of the 1950s, 1960s, and 1970s being in large part dictated by the need to achieve this. Finally, the situation was changed once again by North Sea oil – but this constitutes a new chapter in British economic development which we cannot deal with here.

Cheap food

The economic consequences for the working class of this new economic orientation were also clear. If one had to sum up in a single phrase the one most important economic base of capitalist political supremacy in Britain in the entire century and a quarter after 1846, it would undoubtedly be *cheap food* – cheap food based on the abolition of the tariff on food imports and then cheap food, and other goods, capable of being imported, without a competitive manufacturing sector, through the income from British foreign investments. All else, all the other economic structures, all the ideology, etc., was created on this unshakeable fact that the British working class was given, in the rhetoric of the period, the 'big loaf' of free trade in food as opposed to the 'small loaf' of protectionism in agriculture. When the necessity for equivalent rates of exploitation compared to other countries, to create a competitive manufacturing sector, was also removed by the foreign investments then the economic basis for extremely powerful political integrative mechanisms was created. Cheap food, combined with foreign investment, gave to British capitalism a stability for its political dominance not matched by any other ruling class in the world, except for the United States which created its basis of low-price food not by imports but by the incredible level of productivity of its internal capitalist agriculture.

Finally, if these statements seem excessive or an example of 'economic reductionism', then the following fact should be noted. *From 1846 until 1970 not one single British govern-*

ment with the known intention to place a tariff on imports of food was ever elected (1970 is the turning-point because of Heath's pledge to join the EEC Common Agricultural Policy). In the intervening 124 years an attempt to introduce a tax on food imports was tried twice in elections. In 1906 the Tories appeared pledged to introduce protectionism. The result was, in terms of MPs, the greatest electoral defeat in the entire history of the Conservative Party, with its share of seats in the House of Commons reduced from 60 per cent in 1900 to 23 per cent in 1906. The second time an attempt was made to introduce a tariff on food, in 1923, it led to the defeat of the Conservatives under Baldwin and the creation of the first ever Labour government. Those disinclined to believe in economic and social forces as the driving force of politics need merely ponder that 124-year electoral record.

Finally, of course, once these economic mechanisms, and economic orientation, were put in place then they easily explain the internal balance of forces within, and nature of, the British ruling class we looked at earlier. The great internationally expanding sectors of the British economy from the mid-nineteenth century onwards were not manufacturing, but those based on foreign investment – both direct investment and more especially portfolio investment of the type particularly suited to banking, those with rentier incomes, etc. The rising working-class living standards which this economic system made possible within Britain created a vast new market for the necessities of working-class life – and provided the basis for the food, drink and tobacco manufacturers, retail chains, etc., whose dominance in the economy we have already noted.

While German capitalism was building up its electronics, chemicals, and steel industries based on a tremendous oppression of the working class, British imperialism was building up its foreign investments, and the specific industry and service sectors to supply its internal working-class market. All the fundamental characteristics of the British ruling class in the late nineteenth century at which we have looked flow logically from these features.

Finally, these very same developments evidently also

created the basic potential for a very specific type of social alliance. To have developed an economy primarily based on manufacturing capital in Britain would have required a high rate of exploitation to be competitive. It would have demanded a low exchange rate of the currency to make exports competitive – an exchange rate that would have put up the price of food and other imports and cut the value of funds available for foreign investment. The sectors based in banking, food manufacturing, construction and other sectors supplying the internal market – as well as those primarily engaged in foreign investment – required no such measures. On the contrary, they required a high exchange rate of the currency to finance foreign investment – and that high exchange rate meant cheap imports, which could then be processed by the food, drink and similar manufacturers. Far from needing a high rate of exploitation such sectors needed a large internal market based on a relatively high working-class purchasing power – a policy to which those sectors based on foreign investment had no particular objection as their profits did not come from the exploitation of the British working class anyway. An economic basis therefore existed for such sections of capital to appeal to, and build a mass base in the working class. That alliance was called the Conservative Party. It was all the more necessary because, for all his efforts, Peel *had not* succeeded in halting the crisis of the British political system. He had merely succeeded in enormously prolonging its timescale and qualitatively altering its form. No sooner was the new party system put in place than it began to disintegrate – that process of 'disintegration from the edges' constituting the fundamental dynamic of British politics for the next 120 years. That disintegration was also the reason for the rise of supremacy of the Conservative Party within the British ruling class.

8.

The Curve of Tory Development

The processes enabling the Conservative Party to build up its mass base after 1846, and thereby the mechanisms which led to its decline after 1931, can be very clearly traced. In Britain major economic and social divisions correspond to geographical areas of the country, and constituency results can be correlated against data from censuses and other sources. These facts mean that, even before opinion poll and other studies become available, the social base of Conservative Party support can be traced accurately. This is confirmed rather strikingly when opinion poll and the other modern types of analysis do become available after the Second World War: they correlate very precisely with the earlier geographical studies. We will follow in this chapter, therefore, the actual processes of the rise of Conservative support and in the next discuss the social forces underlying it.

The English countryside

If we take the original Conservative vote of 1847 then it is extremely easy to show its character. The original core of the Conservative Party, the impregnable bastion from which it has never been shifted, is its domination of the English countryside – a domination completely consistent with the original Tory landowner base. Between 1847 and 1865 the Conservatives won between 62 and 75 per cent of the English country seats in every election. The Tories were a minority but significant force in the smaller town seats – winning 28–47 per cent of the town constituencies with fewer than 2,000 voters. In the big city constituencies with more than 2,000 voters the Conservatives were virtually irrelevant, taking only 9–17 per cent of the seats. No clearer picture of a party with its original base in the countryside than the Conservatives can be imagined.

In 1983 the Conservative Party vote in the English counties averaged 50 per cent – 8 per cent above its average in Britain as a whole. By contrast, in the eight Metropolitan counties of England the Tory vote averaged only 37 per cent – 5 per cent less than its average in Britain as a whole. The unification of the English, and later British, countryside under the unchallenged domination of the Conservative Party is the most permanent of all the political conquests of Toryism.

The South of England

Tory strength in the countryside is matched by its position in the South and South East of England. If a line is taken across England from the Humber estuary in the North East to the Bristol Channel, and then extended downwards to the South Coast, the Tories had a majority to the south of that line, excluding London, in every general election of the nineteenth century except for 1832 and 1885. From 1832 to 1865 the Tories *never* had a majority north of that line.

If we turn to the 1983 election then the Conservatives gained 51 per cent of the vote in East Anglia, 51 per cent in South West England, and 55 per cent in South East England outside London. In contrast, they gained only 28 per cent of the vote in Scotland, 31 per cent in Wales, 35 per cent in North East England, and 39 per cent in Yorkshire.

Defeat in Scotland, Ireland and Wales

The three other nations that have historically been within the British state are all areas of fundamental Tory failure. This failure is all the more complete because, at its formation, the Conservative Party commanded very considerable support in Wales and Ireland, inherited from the old pre-1846 Tory Party.

In three out of the four elections between 1847 and 1865, the Conservatives actually won a higher proportion of seats in Wales than in England. They also won a majority of seats in Ireland in 1859. Only in Scotland was the Conservative Party massively unpopular even at its birth – with the Tory proportion of the Scottish seats being only 15 per cent in 1847.

After 1859, however, any semblance of balance in the Conservative position between the different nations of the British state totally collapsed. In 1859 the Tories won 46 per cent of the seats in England, 52 per cent in Wales, 28 per cent in Scotland, and 54 per cent in Ireland. By 1885 they won 47 per cent of the seats in England, but only 16 per cent in Wales, 11 per cent in Scotland, and 16 per cent in Ireland. By 1885 the Tories had become an almost exclusively English party.

If we take the trends since the inception of the Conservative Party then the Tories have been defeated in the vote in Wales in every single election since 1859. In Ireland by the 1870s the Tories had been reduced to a rump holding only the North East Protestant Unionist seats, together with a few supporters of Britain in Dublin. When this link with the Unionists broke in February 1974, the effect on the Tory Party was major: without those seats Edward Heath was unable to lead the largest party in Parliament and Labour came to power.

In Scotland the Conservatives had one period of success, lasting roughly for the first half of the twentieth century. After 1955, however, Conservative support rapidly declined again. By 1983 the Tories gained only 28 per cent of the vote in Scotland – 14 per cent below their level in Britain as a whole. In England, by contrast, the Tories have had a higher proportion of the vote than in the British state as a whole in every election since 1859.

Nothing could be more historically ridiculous, therefore, than the Conservative Party's claim to be a 'British'. as opposed to a merely *English*, party. Apart from Scotland in the first half of the twentieth century, the Conservative Party has never had any serious support in any part of the British state outside of England and the Protestant enclave of the North of Ireland. In 1983 the Conservative Party gained 46 per cent of the vote in England, but only 31 per cent in Wales, 28 per cent in Scotland, and 0 per cent in the North of Ireland.

The English regions

So far, we have looked at areas where Tory success or failure has been constant. The struggle for the English regions, however, is the process which has historically marked the rise and fall of Tory support. This struggle only extended into Scotland at the very peak of the Conservative vote.

The first English region in which the Conservative Party gained support in its rise was Lancashire and Cheshire – the North West of England. The chronology of this was clear. Even in 1859 the Tories won only 42 per cent of the seats in Lancashire and Cheshire, compared to 47 per cent in Britain as a whole. However, by the mid-1860s the number of seats won by the Tory Party in the North West of England was already above its average for Britain as a whole. By the end of the nineteenth century the North West of England had become a gigantic Tory fortress – the Conservatives won 87 per cent of the seats in 1895 and 81 per cent in 1900.

No such progress was made in Yorkshire – to take another key area of the North of England. Only in one election, 1900, did the Conservatives win even 50 per cent of the Yorkshire seats – a freak due to the impact of the Boer War. Even by 1895 the Conservatives could only win 40 per cent of the seats in Yorkshire when they were winning 61 per cent in Britain as a whole.

The second area into which the Conservative Party expanded was London. Here the Tory breakthrough came in the 1870s. In 1859 and 1865 the Tory isolation in London was complete – the Conservatives did not win a single seat. Even in 1874 the percentage of Tory seats in London – although by this time significant – was still below the average for Britain as a whole. The Tory seats in London caught up with the British average in 1880 and then went on to massively exceed it. By 1895 and 1900 the Conservatives won 86 per cent of the seats in London.

The third English region into which the Conservative Party expanded was Birmingham and the West Midlands. In this case, however, the Tory breakthrough was not gradual and cumulative, but sudden and abrupt – a product of the political crisis produced by the 1886 split in the Liberal Party. In November 1885 the Tories had been defeated in ten out of the eleven seats in Birmingham. In July 1886, less than a year later, the Tories with their new 'Liberal Unionist' allies under Chamberlain won all eleven seats in the Birmingham district. From then on, until the First World War, the Tories won every single seat in Birmingham in every single general election – one of the most complete and violent party transformations in electoral history. Not until 1945 did the Conservatives lose their majority of seats in Birmingham.

The conquest of Scotland

The victory of 1886 in the West Midlands, with all its direct and indirect consequences, sealed Conservative electoral supremacy in Britain as a whole. Nevertheless, there was one further area to be added to achieve the absolute inter-war peak of the Tory vote. This was Scotland.

As we have already noted, at the time of the creation of the Conservative Party Scotland was the one area where Toryism had no real support. By the beginning of the twentieth century, however, significant new trends appeared in Scottish politics. Scotland, unlike Wales, proved itself susceptible to the chauvinist campaign of the Tories in the 1900 'Boer War' election. In that year the Tories actually won a majority of the Scottish seats for the first time since 1832. However, the gap between Tory and Liberal votes in Scotland had been narrowing throughout the latter part of the nineteenth century, decreasing from 65 per cent in 1868 to 1 per cent in 1900.

Furthermore, once established, this strengthening Tory position in Scotland continued for a definite historical period. The Tory vote in Scotland was actually higher than in England in 1945, and the Conservatives repeated this in 1950 and 1955. Strange as it may appear today, in the period from roughly the beginning of the twentieth century up to 1955 Scotland was actually an area of growth and strength for the Tory Party at the electoral level.

The Tory decline

The decline of the Tory vote after 1931 is simply a mirror-image of the period of upswing. The only significant difference is that, in the rise, the West Midlands was won by the Tory Party after the North West of England; in the downswing, the North West of England was lost before the Tory position in the West Midlands began to be affected.

Table 7   **Tory percentage of the vote in 1955**

Wales	30
Yorkshire and Humberside	45
Tyneside and North	46
East Midlands	47
West Midlands	49
London	49
Scotland	50
North West England	51
East Anglia	52
South West England	52
South East England	57
North of Ireland	69
Average for Britain	50

Table 7 shows the percentage of the vote gained by the Conservative Party in the different regions and nations of the British state at the time of its post-war peak vote of 1955.

These figures clearly show the cumulative effects of the period of Conservative rise we have just looked at. The highest Tory vote of all in 1955 was in the Protestant enclave in the North of Ireland. After this came the traditional Conservative bastions of Southern England, the North West of England, Scotland, London, and the West Midlands. At the lowest levels of the Tory vote were the traditional Conservative disaster areas – Wales, Yorkshire and the North of England.

Table 8   **Tory percentage of the vote in 1983**

	1983	Change 1955–83
North of Ireland	0	−69
Scotland	28	−22
Wales	31	+ 1
Tyneside and North	35	−11
Yorkshire	39	− 6
North West England	40	−11
East Midlands	47	0
West Midlands	45	− 4
London	44	− 5
South West England	51	− 1
East Anglia	51	− 1
South East England	55	− 2
Average for Britain	42	− 7

Table 8 shows the electoral results for 1983, and the new order of regions indicates the fall in the Conservative vote since 1955. (The figures for falls are slightly affected by roundings of decimals.)

As can be seen, the decline of the Tory vote since 1955 is by no means an even process. In certain areas of the country, Conservative support has scarcely declined at all. In others, it has collapsed – the most striking of these latter cases being the disappearance of the Conservative base in the North of Ireland, the 22 per cent fall in support in Scotland, the 11 per cent fall in support in Northern England and North West England, and, less severely, the 6 per cent fall in Yorkshire, 5 per cent fall in London and 4 per cent fall in the West Midlands. In effect, Tory support has remained virtually constant in its traditional bastions and origins in the South of England, together with certain other areas of the country; at the same time, the areas which the Conservative Party gained in its rise in the nineteenth and early twentieth centuries have been progressively lost.

This trend becomes even clearer if we now turn to the other fundamental aspect of the Tory advance during its period of rise – the move from the countryside and small towns into the big cities. In Table 9 we show the percentage of the vote gained by the Conservative Party in the largest cities, outside Ireland, in 1955 and 1983 and the fall in its vote between the two elections.

Table 9   **Tory percentage of the vote in the big cities**

	1955	1983	Change 1955–83
Glasgow	48	19	−29
Liverpool	53	29	−24
Sheffield	43	29	−14
Manchester	50	30	−20
Leeds	47	35	−12
Edinburgh	55	35	−20
Cardiff	50	41	− 9
Birmingham	50	39	−11
Bristol	48	42	− 6
London	49	44	− 5
Average for Britain	50	42	− 7

The pattern is obvious. In every single big city, except forLondon and Bristol, the Tory vote has declined since 1955 by more than in Britain as a whole. In other words, the Conservative Party originated in the South of England, the countryside and the smaller towns. In its period of rise the Tory Party marched into the big cities and into the North of England and Scotland. In its decline the Conservative Party has been thrown out of Scotland and the big cities, and is in the process of being thrown out of the North of England. Support is, so to speak, 'disintegrating at the edges' – the Tory Party is maintaining itself in its original areas of strength, but losing those which were gained in its rise.

9.

The Social Base of the Tory Vote

The reality of the rise and decline of the Conservative Party becomes even clearer if we now turn from mapping its gains and losses geographically to the social processes which underlie these shifts. If we take first the broadest divisions within the British state – those between the nations which have historically comprised it – then the best available guides to their relative economic and social positions over long periods of time are their respective per capita assessments for tax. Table 10 therefore shows these for periods since the beginning of the nineteenth century. As we are concerned here with *relative* economic position, we have expressed all figures as a percentage of the assessment for England.

Table 10   **£ per capita tax assessments as a percentage of that for England**

	1803	1851	1871	1891	1921	1964–65
England	100	100	100	100	100	100
Scotland	47	72	79	83	110	88
Wales	56	65	63	65	66	84
Ireland						
32 counties		27	32	46	20	
6 counties						64

Source: Calculated from Rose, *The United Kingdom as a Multi-Nation State*, Strathclyde University.

As can be seen from these figures, Ireland has remained consistently by far the poorest nation within the British state. Ranking next after Ireland, but a long way ahead, comes Wales. England has remained, with the exception of one short period, easily and consistently the richest part of the British state.

The one case which shows a change in its relative position over time is Scotland. Scotland started the nineteenth century even poorer than Wales and remained, relative to England, extremely poor until the mid-nineteenth century. But from the latter part of the nineteenth century onwards Scotland's position improved rapidly so that its average per capita assessment for tax actually was higher than England by the period immediately following the First World War. Then a new decline set in: by the 1960s Scotland had again fallen behind England.

The relation of these economic and social unevennesses to the levels of Tory support we looked at earlier is obvious. The majority Catholic population of Ireland, living in the consistently poorest part of the British state, was resolutely hostile to the Conservative Party and to British rule. Wales, the second poorest part of the British state after Ireland, was the other absolutely consistent area of Tory failure from the 1860s onwards. The specific path of Conservative development in Scotland – low support in the mid-nineteenth century, rising support in the period around the First World War, and then a collapse from the 1950s onwards – evidently correlates perfectly with the changing relative economic position of Scotland itself. England, the consistently richest part of the British state, is the traditional stronghold of the Conservative Party. The correlation between relative economic and social position and degree of support for the Conservative Party is complete.

Exactly the same pattern is shown if regional unevennesses, as well as national, are considered. Within Ireland British and Unionist rule systematically built up a comparatively privileged position for the Protestant working class of the North as against the Catholic South. Taking indexes of poverty to illustrate this, by 1891 the number of paupers in Belfast was only half the level of Catholic Dublin and only a quarter that of Catholic Cork, Waterford, and Limerick. Skilled building workers in Belfast, chiefly Protestants, had wage rates higher than areas of England such as Yorkshire, the North of England, and Scotland. From 1945 to 1965 less factory space was built by the North of Ireland government in a city with a Catholic majority (such as Derry) than in a Protestant city with a much smaller population (such as Larne). Prior to 1974 the Protestant working class of the North of Ireland was the most secure of all mass urban bases of the Conservative Party.

Within Scotland the average figures do not show the incredible difference between the West Coast industrial towns, centred on Glasgow, and the other areas of the country. By 1971, the last census for which full figures are available, Glasgow had only half the number of 'upper professional' occupations compared to Britain as a whole, but twice the average rate of male unemployment, half the average level of car ownership, and by far the highest incidence of infant mortality in Britain. By 1983 there was not a single Conservative MP elected from a Glasgow constituency.

In Wales the most basic social division is between the industrial south and the rural north – coupled with a fundamental language question. As late as 1891 the majority of the population of Wales was still Welsh-speaking. In 1961 the figure was still 27 per cent – which can be compared to under 2 per cent for Gaelic-speaking in Scotland. By 1983 the Conservative Party was gaining 45 per cent of the vote in rural Powys, but only 19 per cent in Mid-Glamorgan. Plaid Cymru was strong in Welsh-speaking North Wales, gaining 33 per cent of the vote in Gwynedd.

In England itself the distinctions between the regions are well indicated by comparing wage levels for standard industries between different cities. The pattern at the turn of the century is quite clear: the Tory stronghold of London had the highest wage rates in every major job category (bricklayer, engineer, printing compositor, etc.), followed by the Conservative-dominated cities of the North West of England and Birmingham. Leeds (Yorkshire) and Newcastle (the North East) had low wage rates and were areas of classic Tory failure.

The same pattern prevails today. Average personal income is higher in the South East, rates of unemployment lower and Tory percentages of the vote higher than anywhere else in the country. The Tory areas of support are, with minor exceptions, those with low rates of unemployment and high rates of pay. The famous North–South divide is rooted in an immense social reality.

Opinion polls

If we now turn to the Tory decline after the Second World War then here analysis of geography and social trends can be supplemented through opinion polls and similar types of studies. As all the different types of analysis cross-correlate, there is little doubt that the social shifts in Tory support are being accurately followed.

Looking first at the initial period of post-war Tory decline from 1955 to 1964, Gallup Poll studies show a general drop in Tory support among all social groups: the percentages of the upper middle class, the middle class and the very poor voting Tory all fell by 12 per cent in this period, while the percentage of the working-class vote fell by 8 per cent. Although the social criteria used in these studies are crude, there is no reason to doubt that they show an underlying trend of some significance.

Table 11   **Percentage of different social groups voting for the Tory Party**

	1964	1970	1974 (Feb)	1974 (Oct)	1979	1983	Change 1964–83
Professional middle class (AB)	75	79	67	63	61	55	−20
White-collar workers (C1)	61	59	51	51	52	49	−12
Skilled manual workers (C2)	34	35	30	26	39	38	+ 4
Semi-skilled and unskilled workers (DE)	31	33	25	22	33	30	− 1

This is borne out by taking the more detailed breakdown of

opinion poll studies available for the period from 1964 onwards (see Table 11). The figures used for 1979 and 1983 in this Table are those published for the Harris 'exit poll'. Substitution of, for example, the published MORI figures would give slightly different absolute figures but identical trends. As can be seen, Tory support fell between 1964 and 1983 in every social category except skilled workers. Among skilled workers, Tory support actually increased.

If we want to look at the structural shifts taking place, however, and to ignore the inevitable political fluctuations which take place from election to election, then support for the Tory Party in different social layers must be compared to support in the population as a whole. In Table 12, therefore, we give the difference between Tory support among different social groups compared to Tory support in the population as a whole in elections since 1964.

Table 12 **Percentage support for the Tory Party among social groups compared to Tory support among the population as a whole**

	1964	1970	1974 (Feb)	1974 (Oct)	1979	1983
Professional middle class (AB)	+24	+23	+29	+27	+17	+13
White-collar workers (C1)	+18	+13	+13	+15	+ 8	+ 7
Skilled manual workers (C2)	− 8	−11	− 8	−10	− 5	− 4
Semi-skilled and unskilled workers (DE)	−12	−14	−13	−14	−11	−12
All population	43	46	38	36	44	42

The structural trends shown are quite clear and coherent – confirming that the polls are accurately reflecting social processes. The Tory vote has been lowest, and relatively constant compared to Conservative support in the population as a whole, among semi-skilled and unskilled workers. The Con-

servatives' relative advantage among the professional middle
class, and among white-collar workers, has been eroded steadily and by 1983 was quite low among white-collar workers.
However, the fact that the Tory Party actually increased its
vote among skilled manual workers means that the relative
Conservative unpopularity here had almost disappeared by
1983. Thatcher's unique success with skilled workers enabled
her to arrest – even to reverse in the short term – the structural
decline in Tory support.

Considered historically, however, higher-paid, and in this
case skilled, workers are precisely the mass social base which
the Tory Party had so laboriously built up during the nineteenth and early twentieth centuries. Thatcher, in other words,
has *not* succeeded in historically winning new layers to the
Tory Party; she has simply reactivated the absolute core of its
old mass base. This fact is confirmed by the geographical areas
of support we looked at earlier.

Tory failures

The reality of the continuing social erosion of Conservative
Party support shows up still more clearly if we now turn from
those areas where Thatcher *has* succeeded in conjuncturally
reversing the situation to those where she has had no success
whatever. By far the most important of these is among women
voters – indeed, about four-fifths of the decline of the Tory
Party vote since 1955 can be explained by loss of Conservative
votes among women. From 8 per cent more women than men
voting Conservative in 1955 the difference fell to 5 per cent in
1964, 2 per cent in February 1974, 0 per cent in 1979 and
actually 3 per cent *fewer* women than men voting Conservative
in 1983, according to Gallup polls.

Other studies, for example MORI and Harris polls, still
show more women than men voting Tory in 1983. All of them,
however, show a declining Conservative vote among women
compared to men.

These studies on the sexual composition of the vote correlate
with those on its social composition. In the 1971 census women

comprised only 14 per cent of skilled manual workers, but 39 per cent of professional workers, 44 per cent of semi-skilled and unskilled manual workers, and 71 per cent of clerical workers. The studies showing declining Conservative support among professional groups, unskilled workers, and clerical workers, but increasing Conservative support among skilled manual workers, therefore correlate perfectly with surveys showing the Tory vote holding up far better among men than among women.

A similar trend exists among black workers – also heavily concentrated in layers other than skilled manual. All studies show that up to 1979 85–90 per cent of blacks voted for the Labour Party – we do not yet have figures for 1983. Moreover, a survey carried out for the Commission for Racial Equality found an increasing trend in the 1970s for black people to *mobilise* themselves electorally against the Conservative Party. In 1979 the South East constituency with the lowest swing to the Tories was the Asian stronghold of Southall – with a swing to the Tories of only 0.8 per cent compared to an average in London of 6.4 per cent. In England two seats with large numbers of black voters – Bradford West and Leicester South – actually swung in favour of the Labour Party in 1979. While the average swing to the Tories in Birmingham in 1979 was 6.7 per cent, in the four constituencies with over 10 per cent of black voters the average swing was only 3.0 per cent.

Finally, the most increasingly anti-Tory of all groups, as one would expect, is the unemployed. Here a particularly clear view of the political effects of areas of high unemployment can be gained from the fortunate coincidence that the 1981 census followed fairly rapidly after the 1979 election. This allows a constituency-by-constituency study to be made. The pattern is clear. Only 8 out of the 100 constituencies in Britain with the highest unemployment in 1979 were in Southern England, i.e. in the heartland dominated by the Tory Party. In contrast, all 100 of the constituencies with the lowest rate of unemployment were in the Conservative-controlled South East. The 10 seats in Britain with the highest rate of unemployment averaged a 60 per cent Labour vote in 1979 compared to a 38 per cent average in Britain as a whole. In the same year Labour held 95 out of the 100 seats with the highest levels of unemployment and 166 out of the 200 with the highest levels. Opinion poll studies show that the Tory vote among the unemployed fell by 10 per cent in 1983 – the greatest fall for any social group.

Other layers among which the Tory Party has seen a significant decline in its support are council tenants (Labour led the Conservatives by 27 per cent in 1983), and pensioners (in 1983 the Tory vote fell by 3 per cent – the largest for any age group). These Tory falls in the vote among the unemployed, blacks, council house tenants, and those dependent on state benefits of course help explain the particularly sharp fall in support for the Tory Party in the big cities which we noted in the last chapter.

Finally, we can also see how socially as well as geographically the Tory Party continues to break at its weak links. Thatcher *has* revitalised the old core of the Tory vote geographically and socially and done great damage to the Labour Party. But she has not been able to arrest the underlying social trends of decline in Tory support. The long decline of the Tory vote we started the book with is precisely the underlying break-up of the social alliances on which the old Conservative supremacy was based. Thatcher has been *unable* to halt this progressive erosion of the Tory bloc 'from the edges'.

10.

The Break-up of the Party System

Having shown the social dynamics of the rise and decline of the Conservative Party, let us look at this process within the overall modern British political system. To do so we must go back to the origins of the party system itself. Modern British politics, just as much as the Conservative Party, may be described as the disintegration of stability 'from the edges' – provided it is remembered that the edges referred to are social and not geographical.

If we summarise this development, and at the risk of taking only the chief features of what was a continuous process, then the development of the modern party system may be divided into four periods. These may be characterised, after the initial formative period, as: (1) 1865–85, the loss of Ireland; (2) 1885–1914, the loss of Wales; (3) 1914–45, the great Labour breakthrough; (4) 1945–83, the failure of Toryism. We will take each in turn.

1865–85: The loss of Ireland

The zenith of political stability achieved by modern British capitalism was in the late 1850s and early 1860s. By 1859 both Conservative and Liberal Parties had been created. Chartism had totally disappeared and the chief organisations of the working class, extremely restricted in their numbers, were explicitly reformist skilled workers' unions, tied for the most part to the Liberal Party. Mass independent political parties in Ireland had been eliminated after 1848. From 1859 until 1874 the Conservative and Liberal Parties between them won every single seat in every general election in England, Wales, Scotland and Ireland. The domination of British politics by a two-party British capitalist system was complete.

This monopoly lasted less than a decade. The earthquake which shattered Victorian political stability was the 1867 Irish Fenian uprising. Although the rebellion was itself easily crushed, its political consequences could not be. In 1869 a leading Fenian prisoner, Jeremiah O'Donovan 'Rossa', was elected MP in the by-election for County Tipperary. Attempts to control the situation through measures such as the Disestablishment of the Church of Ireland failed completely. By 1874 the position of the British capitalist parties in Ireland was rapidly disintegrating and in the general election of that year forces demanding Home Rule won 40 per cent of the vote and 59 per cent of the Irish seats. By 1885 the gap had widened to the point where Home Rule candidates won 68 per cent of the vote in Ireland and 84 per cent of the Irish seats. In a mere 7 years, 1867–74, the entire backbone of the position of the British capitalist parties in Ireland had been broken. It was the first great breach in the British two-capitalist-party system – and one that has never been mended.

The loss of votes to the British capitalist parties after 1874 was not vast in terms of absolute size – by 1885 it amounted to a loss of only 7 per cent of the vote in Britain to Irish Home Rulers and 2 per cent to others. But the concentration of the break with the Tory and Liberal Parties in one nation made it decisive. By 1885 the British capitalist parties in Ireland were in a hopeless minority position – a totally illegitimate political force. Their combined share of the vote had dropped from 100 per cent in 1868 to no more than 32 per cent by 1885. Furthermore, by 1885 the disintegrative processes were beginning to spread from Ireland into the British 'mainland' itself – in particular into Scotland (where the combined Tory and Liberal share of the vote had dropped from 100 to 88 per cent).

Indeed, this 'mini-crisis' of 1885 in Britain shows very clearly the social forces that were developing and explains the background of the great split of the Liberal Party in 1886. The most serious challenge to the Tory–Liberal domination outside Ireland was in Scotland. Here opposition to the Tories and Liberals centred on the Highland Land League – an organisation consciously modelled on the Irish Land League. In 1885 the League supported 'Crofters' as candidates against the Liberals and in five cases defeated them – accounting for most of the Tory–Liberal loss of votes in Scotland in this period. New developments in Wales were centred on the Rhondda, where the miner W.Abraham was elected. In England the break-up of the two-capitalist-party system was also in a mining constituency – Camborne in Cornwall. Here C.Conybeare, a radical politician, was elected – officially as an 'Independent Liberal'.

In short, by 1885 it was clear that the two British capitalist parties had completely lost majority support in Ireland and the first small cracks in their domination were beginning to appear in Scotland and the mining areas of Wales and England. Given these facts, it is also clear why it was the Liberal Party which progressively disintegrated under the strain – leading to the emergence of the Conservatives as the new dominant party of British capitalism. Those areas in which the hold of the British capitalist party system were being embryonically or actually threatened – Ireland, Scotland, Wales, mining areas – were precisely those where the Liberal Party had been dominant. The major crisis in Ireland, and the minor one spreading into the rest of Britain, showed that the Liberal Party was no longer an adequate instrument for integrating social support for the British capitalist parties. The social and economic strain was dissolving the links between the Liberal Party and its mass base.

Of the two choices proposed in that situation – Gladstone's to go further 'to the left' and Chamberlain's to move to fusion with the Conservatives – there is no doubt that Chamberlain's was the only effective one. Gladstone's orientation was to attempt to reabsorb and co-opt the rising discontent through a more radical path. This was symbolised in his adoption of support for Home Rule in Ireland and for new positions on land and a general 'radicalisation' of the Liberal Party after 1885. This policy finally culminated in the 1905 Liberal government and Lloyd George's 'People's Budget' of 1909. There were certain immediate tactical successes along this road – by 1892, for example, the Crofters' Party had been reabsorbed – but fundamentally it was a dead end. Social strains were radically decomposing the Liberal Party. Chamberlain's policy, to make social concessions but above all to build up a solid reactionary front to weather the coming storm, was the only practical one. The proof came with the First World War. Conservatism survived the impact both of war and of the rise of Labour. The Liberal Party fell to pieces. The supremacy of the Conservative Party was its ability to weather all these social and political storms.

1886–1914: The loss of Wales

The fact that the 'mini-crisis' of 1885 was the harbinger of things to come was confirmed very rapidly. In 1888 Keir Hardie fought the famous mid-Lanarkshire by-election against the Liberals. In 1892 Hardie and J.W.Burn were elected as Independent Labour candidates. By 1900, in an evident continuation of these trends, the Labour Party was formed and the pre-First World War Labour vote peaked at 7 per cent in January 1910. A second qualitative breach had been opened in the British two-party system to add to that created by the Irish Nationalists. Once more it was areas of Liberal, and not Tory, support which crumbled under the strain. The Tory and Liberal Parties together held up relatively well in England and Scotland prior to the First World War – between them losing only 7 per cent of the vote in England and 4 per cent of the vote in Scotland in the last pre-war election in December 1910. In Wales, however, support for the Tory and Liberal Parties fell by 18 per cent between 1892 and December 1910.

This unevenness of development in Wales compared to England and Scotland can be seen yet more clearly by giving the reverse of the decline of the Tory and Liberal votes, i.e. the increase in support for the Labour Party.

Before the First World War, Labour still remained an extreme minority force in England and Scotland, its share of the vote rising from 1 per cent in 1900 to only 6 and 4 per cent of the vote respectively. Furthermore, the Labour vote actually *fell* in England and Scotland between the last two pre-war elections (i.e. between January and December 1910) – marginally in England and by almost a third in Scotland. In Wales, however, Labour was already becoming a mass party, with 18 per cent of the vote, even prior to the First World War. Far from falling between the two elections of 1910 Labour's vote in Wales continued to advance significantly – from 15 to 18 per cent. In short the success of Labour, and the break-up of the two-party capitalist system, were qualitatively greater in Wales than in England or Scotland prior to the First World War – justifying the characterisation of the period from 1885 to 1914 as that of the 'loss of Wales' in the same way that the period from 1867 to 1885 was that of the destruction of the hegemony of the Tory and Liberal Parties in Ireland. The fact that the 'Irish infection' should spread first into Wales is natural given the social features we discussed in the last chapter.

1914–45: The great Labour breakthrough

In the periods so far considered, the disintegrative processes in the British two-party capitalist system were already clearly beginning to unfold. However, they were still relatively localised phenomena which had acquired a mass character in only two of the nations of the British state. The distinctive characteristic of the period after 1914 was the *general* weakening of the grip of the British capitalist parties – and the first fracturing of the British state with the gaining of independence of the 26 southern counties of Ireland. The motor forces of these processes were the huge election victory of Sinn Fein in Ireland in 1918 followed by the Irish war of independence and Labour's simultaneous breakthrough.

By the end of the war the tremendous fall in support for the Tory and Liberal Parties in Britain as a whole was self-evident – their share of the vote falling from 91 per cent in 1910 to 66 per cent in 1918. Contrary to popular mythology *no* recomposition of the grip of the capitalist parties took place during the

inter-war period. The peak combined Tory–Liberal share of
the vote in 1931 was 68 per cent – not essentially higher than
their 66 per cent in 1918. The peak Tory vote of 1931 (which
we have already looked at) represented a new concentration of
forces within the ruling class but *not* a surge of support for the
two British capitalist parties as such. Indeed, by 1935, the vote
of the Tory and Liberal Parties was in significant decline again
and the seeds of 1945 were already appearing even before the
Second World War.

Table 13 **Percentage vote for the Labour Party in Britain,
England, Wales and Scotland**

	Britain	England	Wales	Scotland
1910 (Dec)	6	6	18	4
1918	21	23	31	23
1922	30	29	41	32
1923	31	30	42	36
1924	33	33	41	41
1929	37	37	44	43
1931	31	30	44	33
1935	39	39	45	37

The more detailed trends can be seen in the vote for the
Labour Party in this period (see Table 13).

Labour's advance continued to be more developed in Wales
than in England or Scotland during the inter-war period – continuing the pre-First World War trend. By 1935 Labour had 45
per cent of the vote in Wales, compared to 34 per cent for the
Tories and 18 per cent for the Liberals, making it the over-
whelmingly dominant party of the Welsh nation. In England,
in contrast, Labour never gained 40 per cent of the vote prior
to the Second World War and its 39 per cent in 1935 was massively below the 55 per cent for the Tories. The vote for the
British capitalist parties in Scotland was marginally lower than
their vote in Britain as a whole. In short, the generalised
breakthrough of the Labour Party *exacerbated* and did not
overcome the uneven processes within the British state.

1945–83: The failure of Toryism

The immediate effect of the Second World War was of course a further fall in support for the two British capitalist parties and a great leap in support for the Labour Party. The percentage of votes for the Tory and Liberal Parties combined fell from 60 per cent in 1935 to 49 per cent in 1945. The task for the British capitalist class was to rebuild its position from that newly weakened situation. Given that Britain is still a major imperialist power, and not a relatively small Scandinavian country, ruling-class interests cannot be adequately safeguarded through a long-term social democratic domination. This has necessarily meant rebuilding the position of capitalist parties.

The progress in this task has been considerable: the Tories, Liberals, and now the SDP *have* in combination succeeded in rebuilding their position in Britain overall since the Second World War. The 70 per cent of the votes in Britain gained by the Conservative and Liberal–SDP Alliance in 1983 is 21 per cent above the capitalist parties' vote for 1945 and even 10 per cent above the pre-war level in the 1935 election. It is roughly comparable to the situation following the First World War.

However, what is clear is that this recovery since 1945 is *not* due to the Conservative Party. On the contrary. The Conservative Party, even in average terms, today is almost as weak as it was in 1945; in real social terms, as we have already noted, it is much weaker. We can see this in Table 14, which shows the Tory percentage of the vote in England, Wales, Scotland and the North of Ireland since the last pre-war election of 1935.

The significance of these figures becomes even clearer if we look at the change in the Tory percentage of the vote compared to the last pre-war election of 1935, the change compared to the Tory defeat of 1945, and the change compared to the post-war Tory peak vote in each nation of the British state (1955, except for Wales when the Tory peak vote was 1959).

The reality of these figures is quite clear. Thatcher's 'triumph' of 1983 is in fact only 2 per cent – 2.4 per cent on more detailed figures – above the level of the Tories' landslide defeat of 1945. This figure, as we have already seen, is on a

Table 14   **Percentage of the vote for the Tory Party in Britain, England, Wales, Scotland, and Ireland**

	Britain	England	Wales	Scotland	North of Ireland
1935	53	55	34	50	
1945	40	40	24	41	54
1950	43	44	27	45	63
1951	48	49	31	49	0
1955	50	50	30	50	69
1959	49	50	33	47	77
1964	43	44	29	41	63
1966	42	43	28	38	62
1970	46	48	28	38	54
1974 (Feb)	38	40	26	33	0
1974 (Oct)	36	39	24	25	0
1979	44	47	32	31	0
1983	42	46	31	28	0

Table 15   **Changes in the Tory percentage of the vote**

	Britain	England	Wales	Scotland	North of Ireland
1983 compared with 1935	−11	−9	−3	−22	−65
1983 compared with 1945	+ 2	+6	+7	−12	−54
1983 compared with 1955 (1959 in the case of Wales)	− 7	−4	−2	−22	−77

descending curve. In every part of Britain the Tory vote is already significantly lower than its post-war peak – 2 per cent lower in Wales, 4 per cent lower in England, and 22 per cent lower in Scotland. Furthermore, we have shown how this conceals greater falls in certain parts of England – and a total disintegration in the North of Ireland. The Conservative Party's support in the big cities is in particular decline. The Tory Party is actually today *already* more unpopular in Scotland and the North of Ireland than in 1945 and, given the rate of descent, the Conservative Party will evidently soon be more unpopular in the British state as a whole.

The reality of the crisis of the Labour Party, the conjunctural revival of Toryism under Thatcher, must not blind socialists to the fact that today the Conservative Party is a party in decay – and has been so for far longer than Labour. The attempt to rebuild a mass popular Conservative Party after the Second World War has essentially *failed* – a failure which inevitably calls into question the entire form of the party system in which the Conservatives were born.

11.

Party Dominance in British History

We are now in a position to come back and look at what underlay all the processes in the 1983 election which we considered earlier. As we have seen, they are not all random or short-term developments. They form part of an immense 137-year party political system in Britain. Once that system, and the dynamic of its break-up, is understood, then everything which has occurred in British politics in the last 30 years makes perfect sense. The driving force is not the crisis of the Labour Party, but the decline of the *Conservative* Party. During the period of its ascendancy the Tory Party could integrate the political fabric of British society in an immense party political dominance. Today it cannot. That underlies all the other political developments.

This is also why the fashionable comparisons which have appeared in the press, likening the present political situation to the period between the wars, miss the essential point. The most fundamental characteristic of the inter-war period *was not* the superficial analogies which are taken up – in particular the division between Labour and Liberals – but the authentic massive popularity of the Conservative Party itself. The votes of the Tory Party in 1931 and 1935 are easily the largest ever recorded by any party in Britain under an electoral system even remotely resembling a universal franchise. The inter-war Conservative governments did not merely defeat the General Strike of 1926, and totally marginalise the trade union movement in the 1930s, but they built themselves mass popular support – no matter how distasteful socialists may find that reality.

Thatcher has built *no* such authentic mass support. Her votes are not the highest but the lowest ever recorded by any Tory prime minister. Manipulations of electoral systems, divisions among opponents, feebleness of Labour opposition, *are not* a substitute for authentic mass popular support. These all distressingly slow down political change, but they will not halt it.

This point can be put even more simply by taking an even longer time-scale than we have done in this book. Here we have studied the rise of the Conservative Party from 1846 and the massive period of supremacy of the Tory Party from 1886 onwards. This period of Tory supremacy is only one of four distinct periods of party political dominance in English, and then British, political history since the capitalist revolutions of 1640–88. These are: (1) 1688–1783, dominance of the Whig Party; (2) 1783–1832, dominance of the Tory Party; (3) 1832–86 dominance of the Whig–Liberal Party; (4) 1886—, dominance of the Conservative Party.

Naturally there can be some argument on the dating of these periods. What is generally referred to as the Whig Party – although it was in fact a loose grouping of ruling-class factions – was in office absolutely continuously from 1715 to 1760 and this is an obvious period of supremacy. Precisely when the Tory Party's supremacy at the end of the eighteenth century should be dated from is debatable. So too is the question as to when the second complete supremacy of the Conservative Party ended. However, all these are details. Each of these political periods is constituted by a central core of almost total domination by a single party with, as one would expect, more fluctuations at the beginnings and ends of the periods. Various transitional groupings from one party to another also naturally exist at the beginnings and ends of periods. But these, too, are only details. The *fundamental* features of each period are clear, as are the curves of party development within them.

(1) The Whigs were already cumulatively building up their supremacy from 1688 onwards. It was they who had decisively opposed the succession of the Catholic James II to the throne and who had been the driving force of the 'Glorious Revolution' of 1688. The Whigs secured a permanent anti-Tory

majority in the judiciary from 1696 onwards and firm control of the House of Lords from 1701. Only in the House of Commons did a fierce struggle between highly organised Tory and Whig Parties continue – in particular in the seven general elections fought between December 1701 and 1715. In 1710–14 the Tories won decisive electoral victories; in 1715 the Whigs utilised the occasion of the succession of the Hanoverian kings, and the Jacobite rebellion in Scotland, to totally destroy the Tories as a governmental force. From 1715 to 1760 the Whigs were in office without a break – their domination became so great that they increasingly dissolved as an organised force into a series of loose groupings. It has been justly said of this period that the Whig supremacy was so overwhelming that they formed not merely the government, but the opposition as well. From 1760 onwards, however, amid the Seven Years' War against France, increasing turbulence unsettled Whig dominance. From 1760 to 1782 a period of political instability and factionalisation, marked by the government of Lord North, set in. This culminated in a great political crisis in 1783 – in which year there were no fewer than three governments. After 1783 a quite different period started with the more than 20-year prime ministership of William Pitt and the emergence of what became a new period of Tory supremacy.

The curve of the Whig Party is therefore a period of rise from 1688 to 1715, a period of total supremacy from 1715 to 1760, and then a period of decline from 1760 to 1783.

(2) The coalition of forces which William Pitt put together after 1783 was originally organised as an alliance of ex-Whig factions and the remnants of the old Tories, initially cemented by massive patronage from George III. Cumulatively during the 1780s, however, starting with the election of 1784, Pitt assembled these groupings into a more and more coherent force. The outbreak of the French Revolution in 1789 formed a solid dominant bloc of the British ruling class against the threat of French capitalism externally and the threat of 'Jacobin' agitation internally. The incredible policies of repression carried out by the Pitt regime internally, and the struggle against them, are chronicled in E.P.Thompson's great *The*

Making of the English Working Class. Edmund Burke's *Reflections on the Revolution in France* is still the best single exposition of Tory–Conservative philosophy of the old school. This savage repression was continued into the nineteenth century and the decade after the end of the Napoleonic wars – by which period the forces put together by Pitt had become in name as well as reality the old Tory Party. We have already (in Chapter 7) looked at the disintegration of the Tory domination amid the great crisis of the late 1820s.

The curve of development of the Tory Party in this period is therefore one of increasing influence from 1760 to 1783, the establishment of Tory dominance and increasing homogenisation of Tory forces from 1783 onwards, essentially total dominance from 1789 until the 1820s, and then Tory crisis and decline from the mid/late 1820s. In the entire period from 1783 to 1832 the Tories were in office for 45 out of the 49 years.

(3) We have already considered in some detail the period from 1832 to 1885. The Whigs, and then the Liberals, won the vote in twelve out of thirteen general elections and were in office for 40 out of the 54 years between 1832 and 1885. The Tories were defeated in the vote in twelve out of thirteen general elections, suffered a catastrophic split in 1846, and by 1847 were a party essentially confined to the rural areas of the country. It took 27 years after 1847 for the Tories to win a majority of seats in the House of Commons, and 39 years for the Tories to win the largest share of the popular vote. There is no problem whatever in establishing the period from 1832 to 1885 as one of Whig–Liberal supremacy and Tory Party subordination.

(4) Finally, after 1886, massive Conservative supremacy was established. The Tories won the largest share of the vote in twelve out of the thirteen general elections between 1886 and 1945. After being a secondary force for half a century the Tory Party was then in office, alone or in coalition, for over 70 per cent of the time in the next 80 years. With the sole major exceptions of the pre-First World War Liberal government, and the post-Second World War Labour administration, the Tories were in office virtually continuously from 1886 to 1964.

Then, after 1964, a new Conservative crisis set in. The Tory
Party was in opposition for $11\frac{1}{2}$ out of the next 15 years. It lost
four out of five general elections. It was evidently to halt this
decline that Thatcher was elected to lead the Tory Party. She
has brilliantly utilised the feebleness of Labour's opposition,
and the undemocratic character of the British electoral system
but, as we have seen, she has been incapable of halting the
decline of mass support for the Conservative Party. The curve
of the modern Conservative Party is therefore a preparatory
period of rise from 1847 to 1886, a period of massive supremacy from 1886 to 1964, and a new period of crisis after 1964. All
the features of British politics we have studied are within the
framework of the break-up of that period of Tory ascendancy.

Political dominance

These facts confirm once more just how little the reality of
party politics, and of British capitalist democracy, corresponds
to what we are taught in the press and at school. There, supposedly, we live in an alternating two-party system, dominated by
'the swing of the pendulum', the personalities of the party
leaders, the 'great debates' between figures such as Gladstone
and Disraeli, the 'fundamental issues' which arise about every
6 months, etc. The reality, however, is that Britain has *never*
had a 'two-party' system in the sense of a stable, alternating,
roughly equivalent dominance of two parties. Those periods
where there has been seriously switching government between
different parties have almost always been periods of transition
from the domination of one party to the domination of
another. They have usually culminated in the split and disintegration of one of the contending parties (e.g. the Whigs after
the period of alternating governments of the 1760s and 1770s,
the Tories after a period of alternation of the 1830s and 1840s,
the Liberals after a period of alternation of the 1870s and again
after the alternation of parties in government in the first decade
of the twentieth century). A series of alternations in government, as opposed to one party being clearly dominant and the
others subordinate, is a symptom of crisis in the history of the

British political system and not a situation of stability. To put it in a rather sharp way, Britain's history is more accurately described as four successive periods of one-party government, with transitions between them, than as one of a real two-party system.

Cleaning-up operations

Naturally again the beginning and end of each of these four periods, as they pass from one to another, is marked by hybrid formations – and we are living through such a period at present. Today's split from Labour to form the SDP, the SDP–Liberal Alliance, and the Tory wet–dry division are all in the long tradition of the disintegration of the Whigs into their different factions after 1760, the split of the Tories into supporters of Peel and supporters of Disraeli after 1846, and the formation of the Liberal Unionists from 1886. However, such fragmentation is simply one of the symptoms of a transitional period between one era of party domination and another and does not alter the essence of the matter.

No matter what Pitt called himself from 1783 onwards he was *in fact* creating the Tory Party. From 1846 the Peelites were going in one direction only and that was towards fusion with the Whigs. Joseph Chamberlain might have called himself a Liberal Unionist: in reality, after 1886 his split from Gladstone created the supremacy of the Conservative Party and he was one of the essential pillars of its governments. In its frivolous moods, the SDP may claim to represent the old Labour Party of Attlee: in reality it is on its way to creating a new capitalist party in Britain.

Finally, what creates these periods of dominance? The answer is simple – although it cannot be proved here but must simply be asserted. Each of these periods of 'one-party government' in Britain corresponds to a specific period of the accumulation of capital. The 1688–1783 dominance of the Whigs is the original period of accumulation of landed, mercantile, and banking capital in Britain. The 1783–1832 supremacy of the Tories is the period of the Industrial Revolution itself – the period of primitive accumulation of industrial capital. The 1832–85 supremacy of the Whigs and Liberals is the period of classical laissez-faire capitalism. The period of Conservative supremacy from 1886 is the epoch of classical British imperialism based on foreign investment – with all the consequences we looked at earlier.

These developments allow the entire history of the Conservative Party to be understood. The rise and decline of the Conservative Party, and of the modern British party system, is a product of the rise and decline of the British imperialist system itself. The reason why the British party system is breaking down is that the immense complex of economic and social forces which made up classical British imperialism are also breaking down. To attempt to overcome the consequences of that, British capitalism must progressively abandon the old economic formulas created in the 1840s and link itself to new and rising forces – in particular, to the powerful European capitalisms of the EEC. This entire reorganisation of the mechanisms of the British economy in turn requires a complete change of the party system. The events of the last 30 years are simply the manifestations of this.

As to what that new party system will be, we can only outline its chief features by name: the formation of a 'Gaullist' Tory Party; the creation of the SDP–Liberal 'pro-EEC' Party; and the creation of a reformist *Socialist*, as opposed to *Labour*, Party. British capitalist politics in the next years – and in the last 30 – is precisely the struggle of that new party system to bring itself into existence. Its aim, naturally, is to forestall any socialist alternative to the long-drawn-out decline of the Conservative Party and the economic and social mechanisms that created it.

12.

The Reorganisation of British Politics

What then are the political perspectives which flow from this enormous process of the rise and now the decline of the Conservative Party? They may be best outlined by summarising very briefly the overall character of the development we have considered in this book.

One simple fact holds the key to understanding the specific character of British society and British politics. Britain is not just any old capitalist society. It was the first great capitalist state and the first great imperialist power in the world. This reality shaped the entire foundations of its society and moulded every social layer which existed within it. It created for the British capitalist class enormous reserves with which to integrate the working class and prevented British capitalism ever having to face an equivalent of the European revolutions of 1848, the Paris Commune of 1870, the German Revolution of 1918–19, the Hungarian Revolution of 1919, or the Spanish Civil War – let alone the Russian Revolutions of 1905 and 1917. The nearest British equivalent to these events – the General Strike of 1926 – was anything but an open struggle for power. Even upheavals on the scale of May 1968 in France, or 1975 in Portugal, have been avoided.

The British bourgeoisie was the first to be able to create what Leon Trotsky once referred to as the 'perfected' form of capitalist rule. By this he meant a system of domination consisting of two interlocking elements: *bourgeois democracy*, a state presenting itself as the representative of the people as a whole but in reality serving the interests of the capitalist class, based on a *reformist labour bureaucracy* controlling the working class and preventing any challenge to the capitalist system from that quarter. This was the final political order which emerged out of Peel's great decisions of the 1840s. The extension of the right to vote paralleled exactly the growth of explicitly reformist working-class organisations in the last half of the nineteenth century. It was a form of rule subsequently emulated, when they had the resources, by every major imperialist power.

The place of the Conservative Party within that political system was also clear. The Tory Party was not, historically, the chief party of the British *industrial* bourgeoisie; that role was played by a section of the Whigs and later, and more centrally, by the Liberal Party. The Tory Party originally represented the most backward, archaic and reactionary forces in the most economically and socially advanced country in the world.

But it was precisely *because* it was a political dinosaur that the Conservative Party emerged as the dominant political party of British capitalism. By the 1840s British capitalism had created two forces escaping its control – a working class that, with Chartism, was beginning to take on a political life of its own and an Ireland that was to seethe in revolt against Britain for a century and continues to struggle against British rule until the present day. To confront these social and political threats to its power, British capitalism had to build a coalition of every possible force in society no matter how archaic, decrepit, or medieval. This need became even more urgent in the 1880s, when British political parties had clearly lost control of the situation in Ireland and were beginning to see a crisis spread into the British 'mainland' itself.

The most resolute resistance to the rising threat of disorder was provided precisely by the most backward and obscurantist sections of the ruling class – the original landlord core of the Tory Party. The modern Conservative Party was built by a process of adding layer upon layer to this nucleus: reactionary Protestant forces in the North of Ireland, the *petit-bourgeoisie*, the military hierarchy, industrial capitalists escaping the crisis of Liberalism. Above all, with the political genius of Benjamin

Disraeli followed by the organising skills of Joseph Chamberlain, a huge working-class base was gained for Conservatism in the more prosperous areas of the country. The enormous economic strength of British foreign investments and British banking capital allowed a stabilisation of this entire political bloc. Domestic manufacturing capital was integrated into it as a subordinate element. From 1886 onwards Conservatism showed itself the stable and totally dominant capitalist party of British society. While the economic base remained firm, Conservative supremacy was unchallengeable.

The *problem* for the ruling class in this system was that while the Conservative Party was able to buttress the political grip of British imperialism over society, it was at great cost to the British domestic economy itself. The specific ruling-class orientation which came to be embodied in the Tory Party – that of international banking operations, foreign investment, high exchange rates and social concessions to the working class internally to maintain its firm political base – constitutes one of the chief historical roots of the present crisis of British imperialism. Internal political stability and a firm base for foreign operations were purchased at the expense of a continuous decline of the British domestic economy.

By the 1960s and 1970s all the international economic contradictions of this system were, so to speak, imploding into British society. Quite new political and economic formulas were beginning to be required. The results were the 'retreat from Empire', the decision to enter the EEC, and, accompanying these, the crisis in the Tory Party from 1964 to 1979 – a period when the Conservatives lost four general elections out of five. This was the period when the social alliances of the Tory Party began to break down; and Tory fortunes reached their nadir in October 1974, when the Conservative share of the vote fell to the lowest level for 115 years and Heath campaigned for a 'national', and not even a specifically Tory, government. It was also a period of disturbance and conflict in British society as a whole, with the movement against the American war in Vietnam, student upheavals, and in the 1970s the largest trade union struggles since the General Strike, and the emergence of

a major new left wing in the Labour Party symbolised by Tony
Benn. All these were political problems of a type British capitalism had not confronted for half a century, and showed the
weakening of the old mechanisms of political integration. The
most urgent political task confronting the British capitalist class
was to put a stop to these processes.

The labour movement

The historical success of British capitalism in politically trans-
forming the character of the working-class movement pointed
the way to a solution to these problems. The British labour
movement, at the time of its formation, was as advanced as any
in the world. For quite a long time, indeed, it was the *only*
working-class movement existing on a mass scale. In its degree
of politicisation, internationalism, development of revolutionary currents and its breadth of support as a class movement,
Chartism – the basic organised expression of the workers'
movement from the mid-1830s onwards – was, in its time,
second to none.

But the huge reorganisation, and international expansion, of
British capitalism from the mid-1840s totally transformed the
character of the British labour movement. It created the space
for the working class to extract economic concessions; to take
advantage of this a huge new, and explicitly reformist, workers'
movement emerged. Its political weakness was complemented
by its tremendous organisational strength, which found its most
developed expression in the power of the trade unions – which
in their size, centralisation, and weight of local shop steward
organisation had no parallel in the world. At their peak in the
1970s, these unions organised more than thirteen million
people. Their leaders were, in the dream of Ernest Bevin and
the reality of Len Murray, continually invited into the 'corri-
dors of power'. The tremendous drive of the working class to
build up its own organisations was locked into a system of
'social contracts ', 'incomes policies', public spending cuts, and
unemployment which held down wages, eliminated social
gains, and alienated the working class from Labour. The great

decline of the Labour Party, it must be remembered, started not in the 1970s and 1980s, when the left began to grow, but in the 1950s and 1960s, when the Labour right totally ruled the party's apparatus and policies. Disillusion with Labour created the first base for Margaret Thatcher.

However, Thatcherism itself was far from the only political force released by the crisis of the Conservative Party from the early 1960s onwards. The decline in the grip of the Tory Party allowed the Labour leadership, under Wilson and Callaghan, to dream of becoming 'the natural party of government'. For the Labour right the crisis of Toryism of the 1960s and 1970s meant that British capitalism should turn to Labour. For sections of the capitalist class, however, it lead to the project of building another party free from the problems of Conservatism, closely linked to the EEC, and able to deal with Labour more successfully than the Conservatives had managed to do. A Liberal Party which had been openly in decline for half a century acquired a new influx of support, interest, and money – the first harbinger of this being the Orpington by-election victory of 1962. In Scotland a similar, if more marginal, role was played by the SNP in the 1970s.

When the Labour Party itself entered into sharp crisis from the late 1960s, new forces drawn from that party could be attracted to the project of constructing a new capitalist party. It was a long line of Labour defections which finally culminated in the formation of the SDP. The disintegrative processes which commenced in the 1960s gave rise not only to Thatcherism but also, logically, to the SDP–Liberal Alliance and to the crisis of the Labour Party. This general reorganisation of political forces graphically confirms that what we are dealing with today are no longer conjunctural shifts but the reorganisation of an entire political system. *That* is the fundamental reality of British politics, of which the June 1983 election is a logical part.

The limits of Thatcherism

If the assault of Thatcherism on the working class is open and obvious, the way in which the SDP and the Liberals fit within the political system is also clear. It is dictated by the previous course of British development and by the character of the labour movement which had been created. Although British capitalism had made immense economic and organisational concessions to the working class after the 1840s, it had used these to maintain a quite unparalleled political domination over the labour movement. British capitalism never faced a revolutionary challenge to its rule, it blocked any possibility after 1917 of a mass Communist Party, it had a reformist Labour leadership which it trusted to be in office alone from 1923 onwards, and it had successfully blocked Marxism or any other revolutionary force as a mass current in the workers' movement.

British capitalism had, however, created a working-class movement that, in its majority, did have profoundly anti-Tory traditions. The forces that created the labour movement had fought the Tories when they were seeking to create the first trade unions in the 1790s and 1800s. They had fought the Tories over parliamentary reform in the 1820s and early 1830s. When the new trade unions were formed after 1850 they attached themselves in practice to the Liberal Party, against the Conservatives. When Labour emerged as a mass party it found its chief electoral opponent in the Conservative Party. The majority of the British working-class movement has been fighting the Tories for 200 years, and to divert it from that course would require reversing that entire history.

The Conservative Party's vote in the working class was large, but essentially passive. Toryism in the twentieth century *never* succeeded in making serious inroads into Labour, or even preventing the rise of the Labour Party vote. Even when Labour's support started to decline from the 1950s and 1960s onwards, the Conservatives proved incapable of gaining support from it – on the contrary, Tory Party support was itself in decline after 1955. Large sections of the British working class have *not* shown themselves deeply attached to the Labour Party in the way that many believed they were. But the working class *has* shown itself historically to be resolutely opposed to the Conservative Party. *Anti-Toryism*, not support for Labour, is the most profound and widest of all traditions in the British working-class movement.

This, at one level, explains why Thatcher has been unable to reverse the underlying historical decline in support for the Conservative Party. It is also why the Tory Party has no mechanisms for institutionalising its links with working-class layers breaking from Labour. The antics of the mid-1970s, with Jim Prior attending trade union branch meetings, were quite rightly regarded as laughable. While Thatcher could, and did, inflict tremendous defeats on the Labour Party between 1979 and 1983 she could not succeed in winning votes for the Conservative Party; on the contrary, 700,000 fewer people voted Tory in 1983 than in 1979. More importantly still, *both* election results were part of the continuing decline in support for the Conservative Party.

Had Thatcher re-created mass support for the Conservative Party, *had* she succeeded in reversing 50 years of Tory decline, *had* the Conservative Party now found some mechanism to integrate in its support the skilled workers and others breaking from Labour, there would be no need for British capitalism to reorganise its political system. British capitalism could rest content today with what it had between the First and Second World Wars – a mass authentically-popular Conservative Party. But Thatcher *has not* succeeded in rebuilding Tory mass support. Simply defeating Labour is not sufficient to create political stability. The 130-year-old party system continues to decline. That is why the levels of support of each party in 1983 formed part of such a coherent long-term pattern of development. It is also why the pressures for a fundamental reorganisation of the political system have not been overcome.

The SDP–Liberal Alliance

Confronted with a working-class movement with profoundly anti-Tory traditions but no equivalent history of struggle against capitalism, in a situation of long-term decline of the Conservative Party, an evident political space is opened. A capitalist party which presents itself as 'anti-Tory', but which in reality is profoundly anti-Labour, has the potential to cut into the Labour Party vote, and later perhaps the labour movement, in a way that the Conservative Party never could. It has the potential to fracture Labour's support into its two historical components – that part which was authentically pro-Labour and that which was primarily anti-Tory. When all the rhetoric is over, this is what the SDP–Liberal Alliance project represents.

Nothing could be more naive than the view that the Alliance is a political expression of the 'middle class'. At its foundation the SDP was supported by John Harvey Jones (chairman of ICI), Clive Lindley (ICL group), Claude Wilson (Rothschilds) and Edmund Dell (ex-Labour Cabinet minister and now merchant banker). The chief executive of the SDP was Bernard Doyle, former head of Booker McConnell. Roy Jenkins is an ex-director of the merchant bank Morgan Grenfell.

As for the election year of 1983 itself, The *Guardian*, on 24 January, noted that the Liberal Party and SDP had recently received £500,000 in donations and that 'The SDP is planning a £250,000 advertising campaign with money donated, it is believed, by Mr David Sainsbury of the supermarket family.' Earlier Lord Sainsbury, another backer of the SDP launch, had noted that 'we are quite simply offering a more stable environment for business'. Of the major firms with annual reports appearing prior to the 1983 election, Thorn–EMI and Marks and Spencer had donated funds to the SDP–Liberal Alliance.

It is worth noting that by turnover in 1981 ICI, Thorn–EMI, Sainsbury's, Marks and Spencer, Booker McConnell and ICL were among the largest hundred companies in Britain. Both Alliance funding and personnel are clearly drawn from the upper echelons of the business world.

The political orientations of the Alliance forces are explained quite truthfully by David Owen and David Steel themselves. They *do* have both tactical differences with Thatcher and points of substantive disagreement on certain questions, e.g. the Trident missile system. They are far more closely linked to the EEC than sections of the Tory Party. But *strategically* they aim to destroy, or at least qualitatively weaken, the Labour Party and not the Conservatives. Owen, Steel, Jenkins, Williams and the others explain this role both in the form of supposedly objective statements ('Labour is finished so the only alternative to Thatcher is to build us') and in the form of the goals they openly pursue ('we intend to replace Labour as the alternative to Thatcher'). In both cases the content is the same. Owen and Steel, needless to say, never explain that they want to replace the Tories as the alternative to Labour!

Within this overall framework the serious voices of the capitalist class can accept, or even consider necessary, a tactically 'left' course by the Alliance; indeed without that the SDP and Liberals cannot aim to replace or qualitatively weaken Labour. The *Economist* explained this clearly in its long-running campaign for David Owen to replace Roy Jenkins as leader of the SDP – a wish granted after the 1983 election. As the *Economist*'s editorial of 6 February 1982 said in relation to the original SDP leadership contest:

> This year, next year or after the next election, the SDP would have had to choose whether its eventual path lay with the reformist wing of a divided Conservative Party or with the moderate wing of a divided Labour Party . . .
>
> Dr Owen . . . could well head a non-Marxist/social democrat grouping ready (with much kicking and screaming on both sides) to realise Mr Tony Benn's worst fears: an SDP–moderate Labour coalition, radical but not union dominated, from which the Bennites are forced to split away. Such a coalition remains the best hope for a realignment of the left of British politics – a realignment which is itself British politics' most urgent priority . . .
>
> If the SDP and Liberals do not win an overall majority in the next [1983] Parliament, the SDP should ready itself for a centre-left strategy rather than a centre-right one. With or without electoral reform the SDP will, if it opts for

the conservative end of the Britain's political centre, be eaten for breakfast by the Conservative Party, as were so many past Liberal revivals. A resurrected Labour Party would then chew over its bones.

In short, the *Economist* wanted no challenge to Thatcher inside the Tory Party, but it was concerned about the danger of 'a resurrected Labour Party'. It considered David Owen, and a tactically 'centre-left' line by the SDP, as the best means to head off Labour. A Thatcherite Tory Party and the Alliance blocking any threat from Labour was the *Economist*'s solution for dealing with the political needs of British capitalism. Consistent with this view the magazine wrote 18 months later, in the chief editorial of its last issue before the June 1983 election:

> We believe Mrs Thatcher and her colleagues should be given a second chance to deliver . . . with the fewest possible Labour (as distinct from Alliance) MPs elected against her – and with an overall majority large enough to do a number of unpopular and necessary things from which a 'tamed' Tory Party would run away.

Having thus endorsed Thatcher, the *Economist* then turned its attention to more long-term considerations:

> It is important that there should still be a believable and democratic left-of-Tory force in Parliament towards which by-elections and a future general election can then swing. It is desirable that it should be of a sort that can form an effective parliamentary force with right-of-Foot Labour. The Alliance needs to feel secure enough at future by- and general elections to help moderate Labour candidates to capture Tory seats in the cities, north England and Scotland; Labour should feel weak enough to give its help to the Alliance in the suburbs, south England, East Anglia and the west. Such a geographical coalition of a southern Alliance and northern Labour seems fanciful at present. The worse Labour does in this election, and the better the

Alliance does, the more possible such a desirable coalition of the left (and the dismantling of the Labour Party under its present constitution) will become.

Another authoritative journal of British capitalism, the *Financial Times*, had exactly similar opinions. In the special editorial prepared for the June 1983 election (which was published in the *Guardian* on 9 June because of the *Financial Times* strike!) Thatcher was given a clear endorsement for the immediate election. The *Financial Times*, however, concluded:

> The policies on which the Alliance has fought the election are not exciting but they are appealing. Its main lines of economic policy we can, with one exception [statutory incomes policy – J.R.], largely endorse – a market economy, its attack on the poverty trap, maintaining European links, and seeking to address the grave problem of unemployment (the major and potentially malignant blemish on Mrs Thatcher's record) through a measured expansion of public investment and employment incentives . . . Its approach to defence and major foreign policy issues is attractive.
>
> In a more representative voting system, the Alliance could emerge tomorrow as the main alternative to Mrs Thatcher, which we would count as a strong gain. This is highly unlikely under the present system; but it would do nothing but good if the underlying support which the centre party has always claimed were realised in the ballot box tomorrow, if only as a marker for the future and a powerful argument for electoral reform.

More important, however, than simply stated positions, or immediate sources of money, is the way in which such political projects correspond to the historical dynamic of British capitalism and the character of its labour movement.

No trade union or Labour Party leader could ever advise their members to vote against Labour for the Tories. Such a view would simply have no impact – indeed it would weaken the position of the bureaucracy itself, because of the opposition it would evoke. But a political tradition of 'anti-Toryism but not anti-capitalism' means that voting for the Liberals or SDP against Labour, above all *left-wing* Labour, *can* be put forward with hope of support.

At its crudest and most openly right-wing level such a position was explained by EEPTU leader Frank Chapple in his article 'Socialism or Survival', which reviewed the election in the *Times* on 17 June. Chapple, who had earlier endorsed an SDP candidate against Labour in Islington, wrote:

> If we had not been so completely tied to the [Labour] party's coat-tails we could have urged our members to vote SDP, or Liberal if they had a chance of winning. Over and over again our loyalty to Labour let the Tories in on June 9.

Chapple also called for the necessity to reconsider the relations between the trade unions and the Labour Party and stated: 'Both wings of the movement will have to be more independent of each other.' Evidently the *Economist* judges the situation very well in believing it can gain support for its line of the 'desirable coalition' of 'southern Alliance and northern Labour' and the 'dismantling of the Labour Party under its present constitution'. It is to such types of trade union forces that Owen and the SDP orientate.

In the trade unions exactly the same pattern will be, and is being, followed as with the Labour vote. A *Tory* arguing for the trade unions to weaken or break their links with the Labour Party is not very credible. But the SDP and Liberals, forming a bloc with the Tories to argue for 'non-political trade unions', is an altogether more serious proposition. Chapple again put it in his usual inimitable style in the *Times*:

> I am convinced that it will not be long before some rank-and-file members start suggesting that instead of giving our money to a no-hope Labour Party, we should donate it to the cause of proportional representation.

Will it never end?

The reason for the emphasis by capitalism on these political questions is evident. The trade unions, and indeed all the other organisations of the working-class movement and the oppressed, *cannot* be defended without the agency of a mass political party. This indeed is why, after many struggles, the Labour Party was created in the first place. There is today *no* mass socialist alternative to the Labour Party, nor is there going to be one in the short term. If capital in Britain could destroy or qualitatively weaken the Labour Party then it could proceed to demolish the strength of the trade unions, the welfare state, and the democratic rights won in Britain in a way that cannot even be imagined today.

Furthermore, the most important step in this attack is not the legal or administrative but the *political* one. Purely legal attacks can always be reversed; they may even incite mass opposition – as Heath found to his cost with the 1972 Industrial Relations Act. Capital must seek to break up the links between the trade unions and the mass political party that is still tied to them. To gain a political credibility and legitimacy for capitalist forces such as the Liberals and SDP is as necessary a part in that process as are the laws of Norman Tebbit.

Even sections of the left wing of the labour movement, using a very different rhetoric, can be neutralised or pulled into such projects of political reorganisation. E.P.Thompson, reviewing the election in the *New Statesman* on 24 June 1983, argued that 'the situation, generally, in the final days of the election could have favoured the strategy of a "popular front" of peace and anti-Thatcher forces'. The practical advice – to vote Liberal and not Labour in some constituencies – was quite explicit.

The *New Statesman* itself carried a special editorial on the election on 27 May, under the title 'Time for tactical voting', arguing for votes for Liberal and SNP candidates:

> The priority . . . must be to deny Mrs Thatcher her goal

of a working majority large enough for her to railroad
through another five years of her new rightism.

Given our electoral system this can only mean tactical
voting to maximise the anti-Thatcher vote . . . given the
present political reality, the hope of an election result
leading to an anti-Thatcher coalition (or at least one where
a second general election would be forced within a short
period) is the only hope available.

The *Economist*, or the *Financial Times*, would doubtless not
use the term 'popular front' or 'stop Thatcher' for their analysis. On the contrary both are explicitly *pro-Thatcher* journals.
But, being serious voices of the capitalist class, they are interested in the substance and not the name. If the *Economist* calls
it the 'desirable coalition' of 'southern Alliance and northern
Labour', and the *Financial Times* in its election editorial even
advised the Alliance to drop statutory incomes policy and
remember that 'Labour's proposed economic assessment might
be more relevant in foreseeable circumstances', then they are
not going to quibble if someone else wants to call that a 'popular front' or even an 'anti-Thatcher alliance'.

The British capitalist class has no fear whatever of the 'com-
munity politicians' of local Liberal Parties, of 'pro-peace' senti-
ment among Liberals (which will always be ignored in practical
politics), of the editorials of the *Guardian* nor even of the writ-
ings of Peter Jenkins in its columns. These are rightly all
treated with the indifference which they deserve. But British
capitalism *does* fear the power of the Transport and General
Workers Union and the National Union of Mineworkers, and
the huge extension of trade unions among public sector and
white-collar workers that has taken place in the last 15 years.
If it can savagely defeat the Labour Party it can proceed to
attack these at will.

There is nothing inconsistent in pro-Thatcherite sections of
the ruling class also wanting to build an 'acceptable' opposition, i.e. one which can replace any Labour Party attempting
to strike out on its own or, failing that, force it into coalition
with the Liberal–SDP Alliance as the only way it can again

come to power. The ruling class of a great capitalist state is not a group of small-time operators placing bets on one party to the exclusion of all others. The hegemony of the capitalist class in society is exercised not merely through its governments but also through the organisation of its oppositions – or more precisely by trying to ensure that as much of the 'opposition' as possible in fact accepts the fundamental framework of capitalist interests, no matter how much it disagrees on particular points. The old Labour Party was acceptable as an opposition, and even as a government, because MacDonald, Attlee, Wilson, and Callaghan could be relied upon to crush any serious left, head off mass movements outside the party, and faithfully maintain the framework, and all essential policies, of capitalism. The role of the Labour Party, from the point of view of capital, was to come to office periodically in periods of social tension, to head off and then demoralise the working class, and thereby prepare the situation for a return to the normalcy of Conservative government. That, in essence, was the system of party political domination in Britain after the collapse of the Liberal Party during the First World War. With both government and opposition correctly aligned, all fundamental capitalist interests were maintained. Within this overall framework the genuine fights which parties had over particular questions even lent legitimacy to the system.

The problem since the 1960s is that *both* sides of the equation have been tending to break down under the impact of the economic and social processes we have outlined. The Conservative Party has become too weak to be able authentically to dominate the country as before. The Labour leadership has been unable to crush struggles outside its ranks and its own left wing. *Socialism*, however weak it may be, has in a real sense grown in strength in the working-class movement since the 1960s. The Labour Party was forced, at least on paper, towards particular policies – unilateral nuclear disarmament, withdrawal from the EEC, questioning of voluntary as well as statutory incomes policy – which are absolutely unacceptable to British capitalism. The very fact that such policies find expression in the field of serious politics, and that they have support in trade unions and a political party which is still a significant force, is regarded as a threat.

Such a situation does not imply, even remotely, that the achievement of socialism is on the order of the day in the short term in Britain. The British ruling class does not believe it is danger of being overthrown today, and it is perfectly justified in that view. But British capitalism, whatever its immediate divisions, can and must operate for the long term. It *does* necessarily seek to eliminate not merely immediate threats to its power but also any actual struggles which might interfere with its major policies, or pose even distant threats to its interests. If there are forces today supporting policies which are unacceptable to capitalism, then they must be pushed out of the mainstream of British politics. Since the 1960s such currents *have* appeared in British society.

In the short term Thatcherism is the response to these strains on the British political system. Thatcherism does not merely provide immediate gains for the capitalist class, it also weakens the entire labour movement and thereby creates a more favourable terrain for whatever is to follow. This is why *every* major section of the capitalist class could support Thatcher's Tories in the 1983 election.

But British capitalism has a far more serious and objective view of the relation of forces in British society, and the trends within it, than is printed in the *Sun* or found in most analyses from the left. The *Economist* concluded its editorial assessment of the election results as follows:

> Britain may still be fortunate. An unfair [electoral] system has produced a government with the strength to carry out necessary changes in an ailing economy, if it can and if it wishes to. But the 1983 election has also demonstrated the weakness of the present voting system. So the system has ensured that there can be up to five clear years of necessary economic changes before the electoral issue will be confronted again. Then it could be the Conservative Party, mauled in what has become the electoral lottery,

that joins the cry for reform which it at present, with more
than a touch of arrogance, spurns.

Sir Geoffrey Howe was careful to warn, immediately after
the election, that the Tories could not expect to stay in power
for ever. Even Norman Tebbit said that he hoped those on the
left of the political spectrum would 'get their act together'.
Such people understand that the capitalist class must organise
not simply its government and tactics of today but also its
opposition of today and its government of tomorrow. Capitalism, in short, must construct an entire system of political domination of which Thatcherism is a crucial, but not the only, part.
No possibility for a socialist solution must be permitted in
either the short or the long term.

That is why, after endorsing Thatcher, the *Economist* talks
of the 'desirable coalition' of Labour and Alliance, and what
gives significance to Frank Chapple's 'we could have urged our
members to vote SDP or Liberal'. It is why E.P.Thompson's
'popular front', as well as the *New Statesman*'s 'tactical voting', completely misunderstand the nature of British politics
today. With the Conservatives weakened, but still by far the
strongest capitalist party, and with the only alternative being a
Labour Party in coalition with the SDP and the Liberals, all
essential capitalist interests would once more be safeguarded.
If that system of parties were put in place then the old 'alternation' of government can be set up in a new form. Were it
necessary to assault the labour movement frontally, the
SDP–Liberal Alliance would form a coalition with the Tories.
Were it necessary to head off and demoralise the working-class
movement then a Labour–SDP–Liberal coalition would be set
up to prepare the way for the return to a Tory (or Tory-dominated coalition) government. In effect, a new party system
would have been created – one quite typical in West Germany
or other European states – and it is this type of reorganisation
of politics to which strong forces propel British capitalism
today. It is this which lies behind all the continuing discussion
on proportional representation, constitutional reform and similar measures.

The labour movement within such a system would be in a very different social and political relation of forces from the one which exists today. With the links between the trade unions and the Labour Party weakened, with the Labour Party reduced in weight and allowed to come to office only in coalition with the SDP–Liberals, with the trade unions themselves enormously reduced in numbers, with a whole series of social gains eliminated, the decline of the Tory Party would be the occasion not for a great victory of Labour but for one of the greatest defeats ever suffered by the British working class.

In reality the point is simple. The enormous historic reserves of British capitalism allowed it to make concession after concession to the organisations of the labour movement. It can no longer afford such luxuries. British capitalism must take back what it allowed to be gained in struggle in the first place. The Tory assaults of mass unemployment and legal restrictions on the unions are not to be counterposed to the political assault of the SDP–Liberals. They are in reality two aspects of the same capitalist need. If Conservatism fails to batter down the defensive walls built during 200 years of working-class struggle against the Tory Party, then new methods will be utilised as well.

The processes we have outlined in this book reflect one of the great laws of politics. Those same elements of any situation which can be used by socialists are also those which confront the capitalist class itself. If the trends and forces at work are not used by the working class for its ends they will be used by the capitalist class for its own. Even the tradition of working-class struggle against Toryism can become, in certain contexts, a weapon in the hands of capital.

The great forces unleashed by the decline of the Conservative Party merely ensure that there will be a tremendous crisis in British politics and society. They determine nothing about its outcome. Those same forces that allowed socialists to make gains in the 1960s and 1970s created the violent reaction of which Thatcherism and the assault on the Labour Party are the expression.

What is at stake today is no longer a conjunctural swing from one election to another but the break-up of an entire political system. In a sense the British political crisis has become a race. The British capitalist class is using not merely an economic assault but also its great political strength to wear down and break up the organisational strength of the working class. The labour movement still itself remains trapped within a political framework which makes it increasingly difficult to defend itself and where its own leadership, and parts of its own left wing, push it in directions that are not against, but in reality in line with, the orientations of the capitalist class. To break out of that situation the working-class movement must face up to issues of a type which are very different to those it has confronted for the past hundred years or more: coalition government, a pulverising economic crisis, proportional representation, the national question, the struggle against the oppression of women, racism, fundamental issues of democratic rights, the fight against nuclear war have been added to the familiar struggle against the Tory Party and through the unions. These and many other issues will decide the fate of the classes in British society and internationally. If the socialist movement does not utilise all the forces unleashed by the decline of the Conservative Party, the capitalist class will.

The British political crisis was not resolved by Margaret Thatcher in June 1983. It has scarcely even begun.

A Guide to Reading

Introduction

There is unfortunately no really adequate single history of the Conservative Party. By far the best from a factual point of view, however, is Robert Blake's *The Conservative Party from Peel to Churchill*, Fontana 1970. For the period since the Second World War, prior to Thatcher, a thorough account is Andrew Gamble's *The Conservative Nation*, Routledge & Kegan Paul 1974. The same author's *Britain in Decline*, Macmillan 1981, contains much of the economic and social background to the development of the Conservative Party and is very good on its origins and foreign policy.

A number of the issues dealt with in this book were originally taken up in articles in the journal *International* and certain arguments are developed at greater length there. In particular 'British Politics in the 1980s' (May 1981), 'The British Crisis' (January 1982), 'Does Thatcherism have a Future?' (March 1982), and 'The Myths of Labourism' (September 1982) all expand material presented here.

Chapter 1

All election results in this book, unless specifically stated otherwise, are taken from F.W.S.Craig's *British Electoral Facts 1832–1980*, Parliamentary Research Services 1981. All figures for the 1983 election, unless otherwise stated, are taken from the *Times*. In this book all figures for 'Britain' include the North of Ireland unless stated otherwise.

It is notable that, rather surprisingly, changes in the right to vote, with a few exceptions, seem to have made only small differences to the electoral trends either in Britain as a whole or in specific regions and nations. *Why* is of course a matter for debate, but this is the reason we have not dealt with them in detail here.

Chapter 2

There are a good many books factually on the long-term development of support for the Labour Party. The best modern one is probably Dennis Kavanagh (ed.), *The Politics of the Labour Party*, George Allen & Unwin 1982. A useful study of the Liberal Party can be found in H.M.Drucker (ed.), *Multi-Party Britain*, Macmillan 1979.

Chapters 3 and 4

Regular material on the composition of Conservative Cabinets, and the background of Conservative MPs, can be found in *Labour Research*. The basic data for the twentieth century in this book is taken from Zig Layton-Henry (ed.), *Conservative Party Politics*, Macmillan 1980, which is a very good factual guide. For the nineteenth century much material can be found in Martin Pugh's *The Making of Modern British Politics 1867–1939*, Blackwell 1982. The figures for Conservative and Labour MPs in this chapter are calculated from David Butler and Dennis Kavanagh's *The British General Election of 1979*, Macmillan 1980. The analysis of the House of Commons of 1841–47 is calculated from studies made by W.O.Aydelotte in G.Kitson Clark's *The Making of Victorian England*, Methuen 1980, which is still a good guide to the mid-nineteenth century. The facts concerning ducal families, as well as much incidental information, can be found in Anthony Sampson's *Anatomy of Britain*, Hodder & Stoughton 1962 – the first and the best of the four editions of this book.

The international comparisons are chiefly drawn from W.Guttsman's 'Elite Recruitment and Political Leadership in Britain since 1950', in Ivor Crewe (ed.), *British Political Sociology Yearbook*, Croom Helm 1974, and Zig Layton-Henry (ed.), *Conservative Politics in Western Europe*, Macmillan 1982.

Chapter 5

A superbly thorough study of the history of British political funding can be found in Michael Pinto-Duschinsky's *British Political Finance 1830–1980*, American Enterprise Institute 1981. Most of the historical material on Conservative Party finances is drawn from this source. The contemporary material is calculated from the regular and absolutely invaluable studies of the Labour Research Department published in *Labour Research*. All calculations on the weight of economic sectors are made from *National Income and Expenditure 1982 Edition*, HMSO 1982.

Chapter 6

A very good survey of the chief data on the British ruling class is in John Scott's *The Upper Classes*, Macmillan 1982, from which much of the data here is calculated. This needs to be supplemented by an economic history and the clearest is Peter Mathias's *The First Industrial Nation*, Methuen 1980. Even more important factually, but much more difficult to read, are P.Deane and W.Cole's *British Economic Growth 1688–1959*, Cambridge University Press 1980, and R.C.O.Matthew, C.H.Feinstein, and J.C.Odling-Smee's *British Economic Growth 1856–1973*, Oxford University Press 1982.

Chapter 7

The 1840s are by far the most important decade of modern British history. Tom Nairn's 'The Fateful Meridian', in *New Left Review* (60), highlights its significance very well as does Gamble's *Britain in Decline*, Macmillan 1981. The classic study of the early political consequences of industrialisation is Edward Thompson's *The Making of the English Working Class*, Penguin 1968. A particularly clear history of Ireland in this period can be found in D.R.O'Connor Lysaght's *The Republic of Ireland*, Mercier 1970.

The 'cultural' consequences for the ruling class of the choices of the 1840s are studied in Martin Wiener's *English Culture and the Decline of the Industrial Spirit 1850–1980*, Cambridge University Press 1982.

Chapter 8

An extremely valuable study of variations in support for the Conservative Party in the nineteenth century is in Robert Blake's *The Conservative Party from Peel to Churchill*, Fontana 1970. An absorbing analysis, almost overwhelming in its factual material, is Henry Pelling's *Social Geography of British Elections 1885–1910*, Macmillan 1967.

For the post-Second World War period the standard studies are those produced for every election since 1945 by researchers associated with Nuffield College. Since 1951 these have been produced for each election by David Butler and various co-authors and published by Macmillan. All the regional information for the post-war period is calculated from these sources.

It should be noted that the regions defined in the Nuffield studies have changed periodically. Prior to 1979 the changes are small and the adjustments are easy to calculate from the constituency results. However, the huge reorganisation of boundaries before the 1983 election makes this impossible. The figures for 1983 used in this chapter are therefore taken from the *Sunday Times* (12 June 1983). Comparison of these with the regions defined for the 1979 election shows that the only really substantive differences for the Tory Party results are those for the North of England, Yorkshire and Humberside, and the

East Midlands. In particular the changes probably understate the fall in the Tory vote in the East Midlands compared to the previous regional divisions. In no cases, however, are the basic trends affected by these changes in regional boundaries.

Chapter 9

The figures on national economic inequality in the British state are calculated from Richard Rose's *The United Kingdom as a Multi-National State*, Strathclyde University 1970. The figures for historical regional inequality are chiefly taken from Geoff Bell's *The Protestants of Ulster*, Pluto Press 1976 – which is excellent for the Tory link with the North of Ireland. Those for the modern period are calculated from L.J.Shapre, 'The Labour Party and the Geography of Inequality: A Puzzle', in Dennis Kavanagh (ed.), *The Politics of the Labour Party*, George Allen & Unwin 1982. The opinion poll studies are calculated from those given in the various Nuffield studies of the general elections and from figures published in *Labour Weekly* (17 June 1983). The figures for votes for the Tory Party among women are calculated from those in Monica Charlot, 'Women and Elections in Britain', in Howard Penniman (ed.), *Britain at the Polls, 1979*, American Enterprise Institute 1981. Those for black voters are taken from Muhammad Anwar's *Ethnic Minorities and the General Election 1979*, Commission for Racial Equality 1980.

Chapter 10

Tom Nairn's *The Breakup of Britain*, Verso Editions 1981, is the most stimulating study of the national dimension in British politics. As regards interpretation of post-war British politics, including Thatcher, there is now a vast literature. Stuart Hall and Martin Jacques (eds), *The Politics of Thatcherism*, Lawrence and Wishart 1983, is the chief collection of essays which attempts to portray That-cherism as a political force not rooted in the specific economic needs and features of British capital. John Ross's *The Profits of Thatcherism*, New Left Books (forthcoming 1984) is a rebuttal of that line of argument. Andrew Glyn and John Harrison's *The British Economic Disaster*, Pluto Press 1980, is the best study of the overall economic policies of Thatcherism.

Chapter 11

There is no full-length historical study of the British party system. In addition to books already cited, we have drawn in particular from W.A.Speck's *Tory and Whig, the Struggle in the Constituencies 1701–1715*, Macmillan 1970, Roy Porter's *English Society in the Eighteenth Century*, Penguin 1983, and Richard Shannon's *The*

Crisis of Imperialism 1865–1915, Paladin 1976. Marx's views on English history are looked at in John Ross's 'Marx on England', in *International* (January 1983).

The two most important modern studies of the general course of English history are Perry Anderson's 'Origins of the Present Crisis', in *New Left Review* (23), and E.P.Thompson's 'The Peculiarities of the English', reprinted in *The Poverty of Theory*, Merlin 1978. Thompson's is the classic Labourist interpretation of English history.

Chapter 12

An excellent guide to the most recent period of the British labour movement is Alan Freeman's *The Benn Heresy*, Pluto Press 1982. The most important recent article on socialist strategy in the advanced capitalist countries is Perry Anderson's 'The Antinomies of Antonio Gramsci' in *New Left Review* (100).

For the international context, which is vital to understand modern British politics, the most up-to-date book on the economic and political crisis is Riccardo Parboni's *The Dollar and its Rivals*, New Left Books 1981. A more overall view is found in Ernest Mandel's *The Second Slump*, New Left Books 1978.